LAWNS AND GROUNDCOVERS

Produced by Meredith Publishing Services, 1912 Grand Avenue, Des Moines, IA 50309-3379 for The Scotts Company, 14111 Scottslawn Road, Marysville, OH 43041.

Dear Friend,

In the late 1950s, The Scotts Company ran an advertisement featuring a homeowner with a Scotts® lawn-fertilizer spreader. The headline announced that this was a "Man With a Plan!" We wanted to let people know that the most foolproof way to have a beautiful lawn was to follow a plan that provided feedings, weedings, waterings, and other basics throughout the growing season. My wife, Nancy, and I have been following that great advice on our own lawn for the 23 years I've been here at Scotts. All of those years, though, we've wished someone would come along and tell us how we could attractively integrate our lawn with the rest of our landscape. Now we can—and you can, too—with the Scotts *See & Do Solutions*™ series of lawn and garden books.

These books fit well with the philosophy Scotts has always embraced: making lawn and garden care a breeze. Each 128-page book presents 50 easy-to-follow plans designed to help you solve the challenges in your own yard. To help meet your needs, every plan is suited to sunny or shady conditions, climate, location in the yard, or a specific landscaping situation. Each plan gives you an illustrated garden map and a "recipe" you can follow to get the effect you see in the full-color photograph—complete with an "ingredient" list that tells you exactly how many of each plant you'll need. Scotts has done all of the planning, so you don't have to. Having a beautiful yard couldn't be any easier!

With this book in hand, you, too, are now a person with a plan. Happy gardening!

Tadd C. Seitz
Chairman, The Scotts Company

P.S. We'd love to hear from you. Call us at 1-800-543-TURF with your questions.

Contents

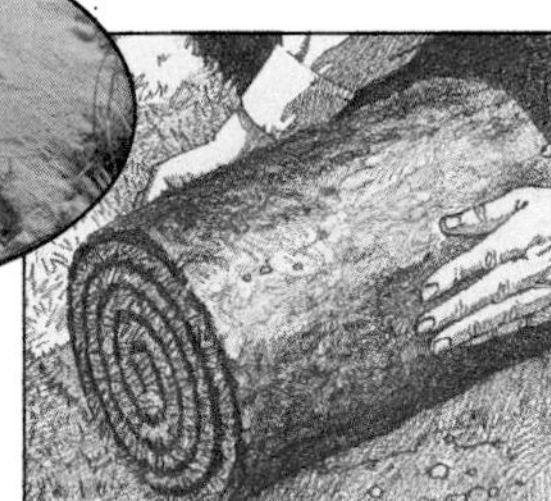

On the cover:
See pages 18 and 19

How to Use This Book

THIS BOOK WAS DESIGNED WITH BUSY GARDENERS IN MIND. WE KNOW THAT YOU WANT a beautiful yard, but don't necessarily have the time to dissect a difficult-to-read volume. That's why we made it simple. These pages explain the easy-to-use features of this book.

What sets this book apart are the 50 beautiful garden plans featured on pages 6-103. A sample of one of those pages is shown on the opposite page.

Many of the book's remaining sections are designed to equip you with the additional know-how you might need to install the plans in your own yard. For example, in the back of the book is a Lawn and Groundcover Basics section that gives you the how-to knowledge you need to plant and maintain the landscapes described in the plans.

On pages 118 and 119, you'll find answers to the most commonly asked questions about lawn care. And on pages 120-123, you'll find the Plant Alternatives section—a listing of replacement plants that are hardy in regions other than those listed on the plan pages. This makes it possible for you to use nearly all of the plans, no matter where you live. If you're stumped by one of the common names shown on the plans, use the index to find the corresponding botanical name.

As an additional feature, on each plan page we've left some space to let you write notes about your garden. And in the very back of the book is a handy pocket to hold notes, seed packets, or garden-plant tags.

As a special gift from Scotts® to get your gardening off to the right start, we've included certificates on pages 127 and 128 for savings on a selection of Scotts high-quality lawn and gardening products at your local Scotts retailer.

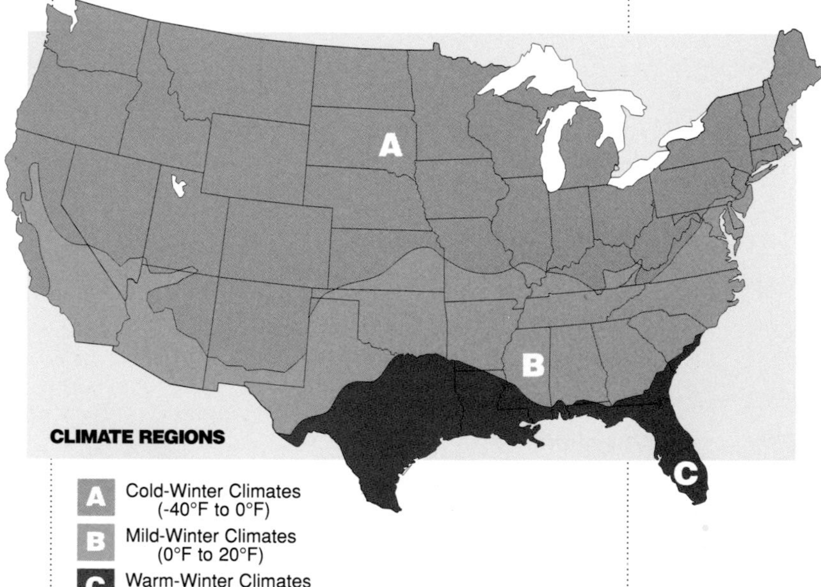

The three regions shown on this **climate-region map** refer to cold-, mild-, and warm-winter climates. The temperatures shown in the key are minimum annual temperatures. With your region in mind, you'll quickly be able to access the plans in this book that—as shown—fit your area. Or, use your region designation and the listings on pages 120-123 to find alternatives to the plants shown.

The **question-and-answer** format identifies real problems just like the kind you may well have in your yard. The question asks how to solve it, and the answer tells you how. It also presents some alternative suggestions.

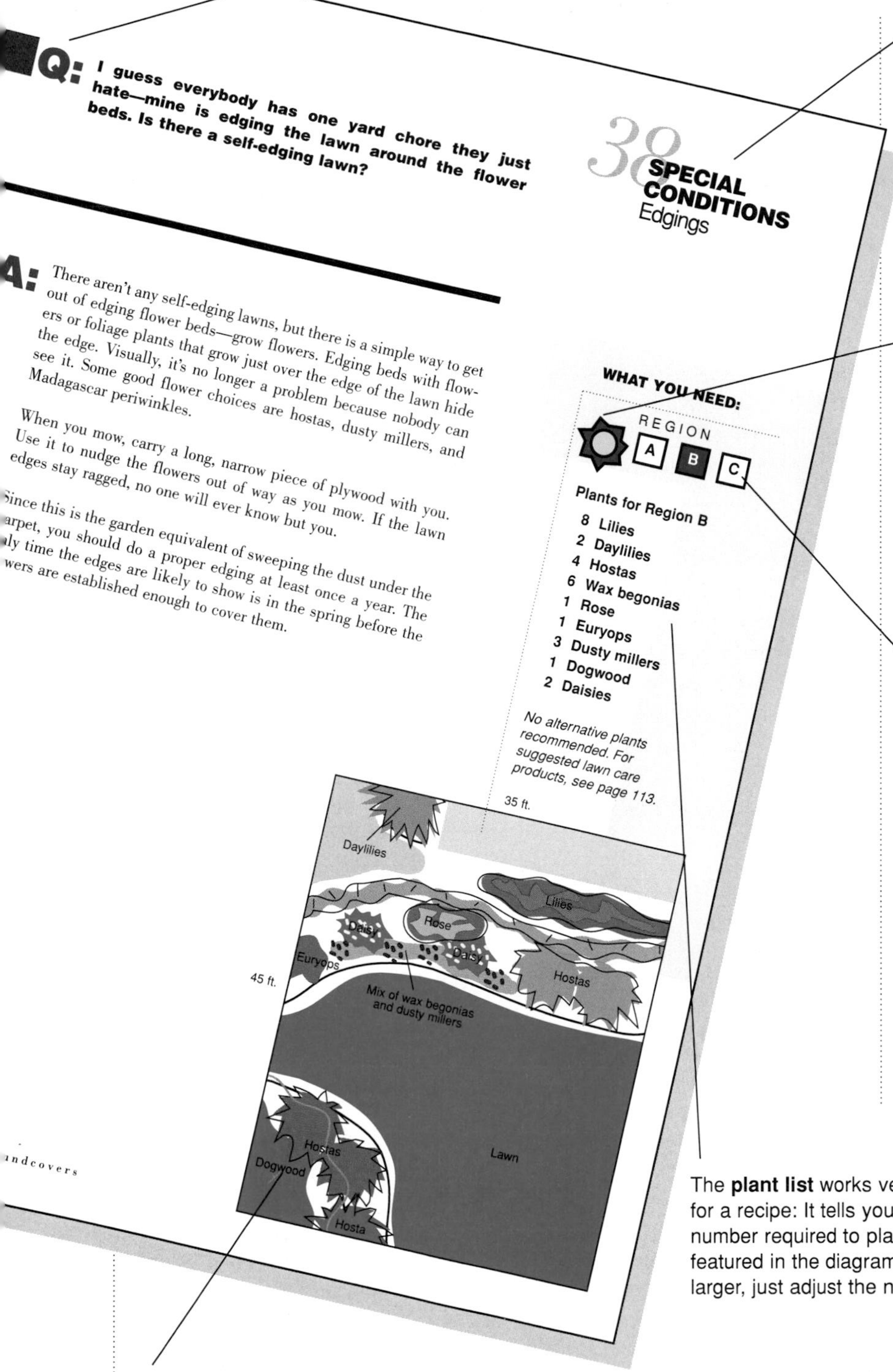

Q: I guess everybody has one yard chore they just hate—mine is edging the lawn around the flower beds. Is there a self-edging lawn?

38 **SPECIAL CONDITIONS**
Edgings

The **headlines** in the upper corner of each plan page help you quickly tell if a plan fits your needs.

A: There aren't any self-edging lawns, but there is a simple way to get out of edging flower beds—grow flowers. Edging beds with flowers or foliage plants that grow just over the edge of the lawn hide the edge. Visually, it's no longer a problem because nobody can see it. Some good flower choices are hostas, dusty millers, and Madagascar periwinkles.

When you mow, carry a long, narrow piece of plywood with you. Use it to nudge the flowers out of way as you mow. If the lawn edges stay ragged, no one will ever know but you.

ince this is the garden equivalent of sweeping the dust under the arpet, you should do a proper edging at least once a year. The ly time the edges are likely to show is in the spring before the wers are established enough to cover them.

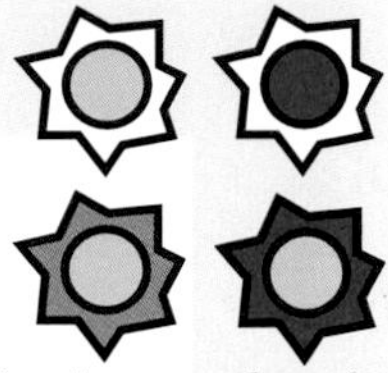

A yellow **sun icon** indicates that the plan is suited for sun conditions. A light blue-and-yellow sun icon indicates that the plan is suited for sun and light shade. A dark blue-and-yellow sun icon indicates that the plan is suited for sun and shade. If the sun icon is all dark blue, the plan is suited to a shady garden.

WHAT YOU NEED:

REGION
A B C

Plants for Region B
- 8 Lilies
- 2 Daylilies
- 4 Hostas
- 6 Wax begonias
- 1 Rose
- 1 Euryops
- 3 Dusty millers
- 1 Dogwood
- 2 Daisies

No alternative plants recommended. For suggested lawn care products, see page 113.

These **lettered boxes** correspond to our three climate regions. The "A" box is for cold-winter climates; the "B" box is for mild-winter climates; and the "C" box is for warm-winter climates. On each plan, one or more of these boxes will be green, telling you that plan is suited to those particular regions. Don't forget to check the Plant Alternatives section on pages 120-123. With the help of these lists, nearly all of the plans are adaptable to any region of the country.

35 ft.
45 ft.
Daylilies
Lilies
Rose
Daisy
Daisy
Euryops
Hostas
Mix of wax begonias and dusty millers
Hostas
Dogwood
Lawn
Hosta

andcovers

The **plant list** works very much like the ingredient list for a recipe: It tells you the plants you'll need and the number required to plant a garden the size of the one featured in the diagram. If your space is smaller or larger, just adjust the number of plants accordingly.

The **garden-plan illustration** is a to-scale, overhead view of the garden featured in the photograph. It clearly shows you how to lay out your garden to get the kinds of effects you see in the photograph. Remember, the gardens in the photographs have been cultivated over a number of years. Follow our plans and be patient. You'll get there, too.

1 SHOWPLACE AREAS
Lawns and Borders

Q: Our back yard is level and has several large trees. My husband wants a beautiful lawn, I want lots of flowers, and our children want a place for summer picnics. Is there any way to satisfy everybody?

A: Take full advantage of that level yard by putting in a large lawn. The best choice would be a grass mixture that will grow in both sun and shade, such as Scotts® Family® seed mixture for Region A, Scotts Aztec seed mixture in Region B, or St. Augustinegrass in Region C. Curve the lawn around the trees, so surface roots don't interfere with lawn mowing and lawn mowers don't damage tree trunks.

Flowering shrubs, such as azaleas, rhododendrons, and camellias, all grow well under trees (depending on your climate) and provide a fine display of flowers. Small spring-flowering trees, such as dogwood, also grow well in filtered light. In the sunny areas, plant a mixed annual-and-perennial border in the sunny area filled with sun-loving plants, such as roses, asters, daisies, petunias, and marigolds, for flowers all summer long.

WHAT YOU NEED:

REGION

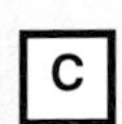

Plants for Region B

- **2 Dogwoods**
- **2 Azaleas**
- **1 Japanese cedar**
- **8 Ferns**
- **12 Daffodils**
- **3 Astilbe**
- **6 Hostas**

Regional plant alternatives listed on pages 120-123. For suggested lawn care products, see page 113.

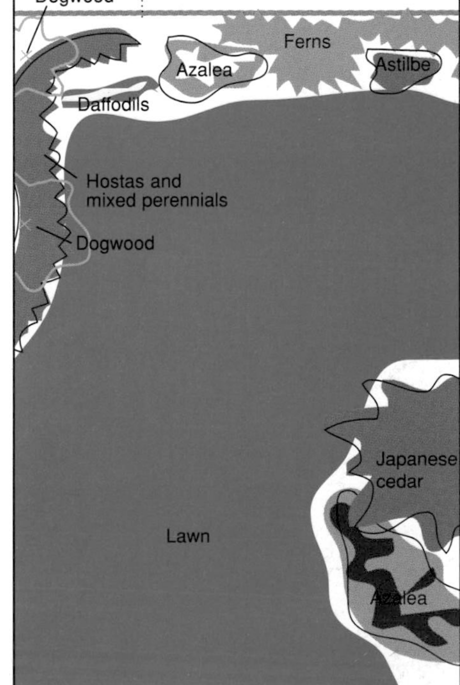

Q: The entry to our house is dull. It's a level yard in full sun. What can we do to create a dramatic effect all year long?

A: Consider putting in a prize-winning dark green hybrid bermuda turf, such as Scotts® Sonesta Bermudagrass, which is perfect for warm climates. Create year-round interest with an island bed of evergreens selected for their bold shapes, strong color, and textural contrast: bright yellow, mottled green, blue-green, and black-green; softly rounded and sharply pointed; thick-leaved and feathery. These are permanent plantings that require little attention beyond normal garden watering and fertilizing.

Put in a gracefully curved border of bright annuals in front of the house and along the side, filled with tall dahlias, pinks, candytuft, and ageratum. By using annuals, you can change the combination of flowers every season or every year, creating a series of dramatically different looks. For fall, fill the borders with a variety of chrysanthemums; for winter, do a show of red poinsettias; for spring and summer, put in tall yellow African marigolds and deep purple petunias. The seasonally shifting show will capture everyone's attention.

WHAT YOU NEED:

REGION

Plants for Regions B & C

- 10 Dahlias
- 8 Pinks (dianthus)
- 20 Ageratums
- 20 Candytufts
- 5 Junipers
- 1 Dwarf balsam fir
- 1 Dwarf cedar
- 3 False cypresses
- 1 Dwarf gold-leaved arborvitae
- 1 Bird's-nest spruce

Regional plant alternatives listed on pages 120-123. For suggested lawn care products, see page 113.

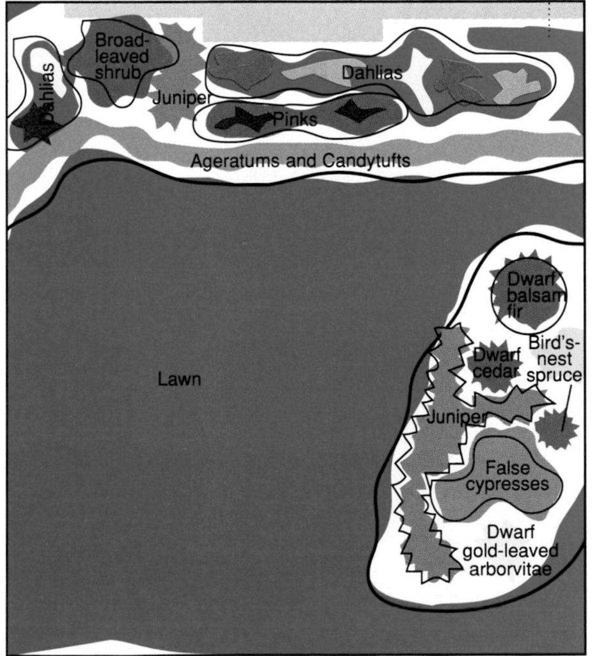

SHOWPLACE AREAS
Lawns and Borders

Q: I have a back yard that adjoins the neighbors' yards on three sides. More than anything, I want my back yard to be a private retreat, a place where I can sit quietly and read, surrounded by greenery. What can I do when the yard is so exposed?

WHAT YOU NEED:

REGION

Plants for Region B
15 Cotoneasters
36 St. John's-wort
24 Ajuga

Regional plant alternatives listed on pages 120-123. For suggested lawn care products, see page 113.

A: Create visual privacy by blocking the view of the neighbors' yards with trees and large shrubs. Maples provide summer shade and brilliant fall color, and they let light in during the winter. If you want a carpet of green, put in a lawn that thrives in shade, such as Scotts® Shady grass seed in Region A or Scotts Classic Estates® in Region B.

Like trees, large shrubs absorb a great deal of sound. Flowering shrubs, such as mock orange and lilac, offer both flowers and fragrance. Holly, cotoneaster, and firethorn provide bright red berries that attract birds and give winter color.

An island bed with low groundcovers makes a good textural contrast to the smooth green of the lawn. Consider yellow-flowered St. John's-wort bordered by blue-flowering ajuga. Another interesting combination might be lady's mantle bordered by sweet violets.

Mark the line between the lawn and the shrubs with low-growing flowers for additional color. An easy-to-grow effect for partial shade is white daffodils ('Mt. Hood') overplanted with pale pink impatiens. The daffodils bloom in the spring, followed by masses of impatiens all through summer into fall.

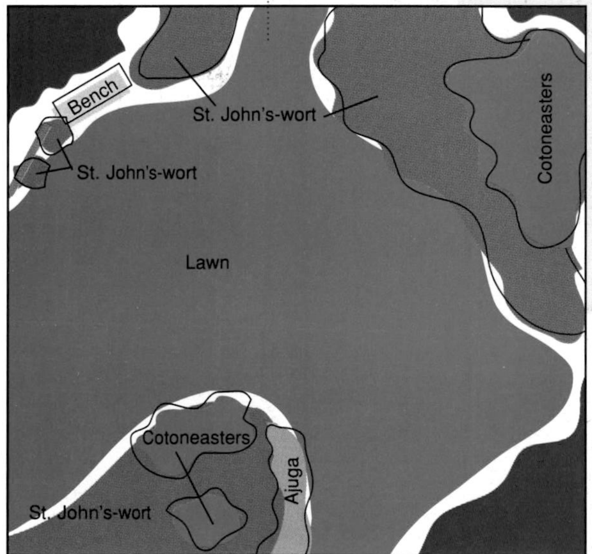

4 SHOWPLACE AREAS
Lawns and Borders

Q: I would love to have a classic perennial border. The only place it could go is in the front yard, but the front yard isn't very big. I'm confused about what to do, since all parts of the yard get both sun and shade. How do I reconcile the double dilemma of small space plus variable light?

A: Use a lawn to create a sense of space and openness, and to dispel the impression of limited space. A good grass for your area might be a tall fescue variety. If you want an instant effect, lay down sod. If you prefer to seed the lawn, consider Scotts® Classic Estates®.

The perennial border you long for can be used to draw the eye across the lawn, again creating the effect of greater space. It can also serve as a way to separate your property from your neighbors', giving pleasure to all of you. Incorporate lots of different kinds of roses into your perennial border: antique roses, climbing roses, grandiflora roses, and hybrid tea roses, for example. Fill in around out-of-bloom perennials with annuals, such as larkspur and snapdragons, for continuous spring and summer color. Set off the entrance to the house with a mixed-bulb bed featuring bearded iris, gladiolus, ranunculus, and anemone. These flowers are excellent for cutting, so you can fill the house with bouquets as well as enjoy them in the garden.

30 ft.

63 ft.

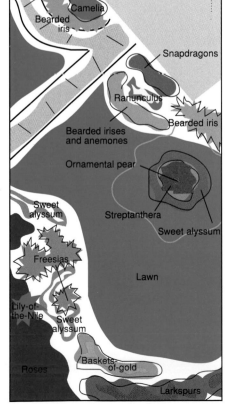

Camelia
Bearded iris
Snapdragons
Ranunculus
Bearded iris
Bearded irises and anemones
Ornamental pear
Sweet alyssum
Streptanthera
Sweet alyssum
Freesias
Lawn
Lily-of-the-Nile
Sweet alyssum
Roses
Baskets-of-gold
Larkspurs

WHAT YOU NEED:

REGION

 A  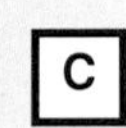

Plants for Region B

- **1 Ornamental pear**
- **24 Sweet alyssum**
- **4 Climbing roses**
- **6 Snapdragons**
- **8 Ranunculus**
- **6 Bearded irises**
- **24 Anemones**
- **3 Larkspurs**
- **12 Streptantheras**
- **3 Baskets-of-gold**
- **2 Lily-of-the-Nile**
- **2 Camellias**
- **6 Freesias**

Regional plant alternatives listed on pages 120-123. For suggested lawn care products, see page 113.

Q: My husband and I both work. We'd love to have an attractive back yard, but our time to garden is limited to weekends. Despite fairly cold winters, we'd still like a touch of year-round green and, of course, some flowers in the spring and summer. Is there any way we can accomplish this?

A: Start with a lawn seeded with Scotts® Picture® grass seed mixture. It contains improved varieties of Kentucky bluegrass and perennial ryegrass that are naturally insect- and disease-resistant. That means less work for you. In Region B, substitute Scotts Classic Estates® tall fescue seed blend.

Plant a small flowering tree, such as dogwood or flowering cherry, for dramatic spring bloom and pleasant summer shade.

Enclose a portion of the lawn with a boxwood hedge to create the feeling of outdoor "rooms" with interesting corners and crannies. The boxwood stays green year-round—a special pleasure during a long, chilly winter. The hedge will need trimming once or twice a year, but that only represents a few hours of your time.

Plant flowering shrubs and perennials for spring and summer color. The nice thing about perennials is that you need to plant them only once, and they will grow bigger and bloom reliably every year. Good choices are bulbs, such as tulip, daffodil, and hyacinth, for early spring flowers; and helleborus, azalea, peony, and Japanese anemone for bloom through fall. Once these are planted, your gardening chores are restricted to normal watering, fertilizing, and grooming. With a watering system on a timer, even the watering ceases to be a chore. Fertilizing and grooming should take no more than a few hours a month.

WHAT YOU NEED:

REGION

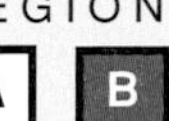

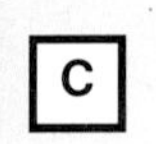

Plants for Region B

- **8 Boxwoods**
- **1 Peony**
- **20 Phlox**
- **18 Tulips**
- **6 Azaleas**
- **2 Daylilies**
- **3 Celandine**

Regional plant alternatives listed on pages 120-123. For suggested lawn care products, see page 113.

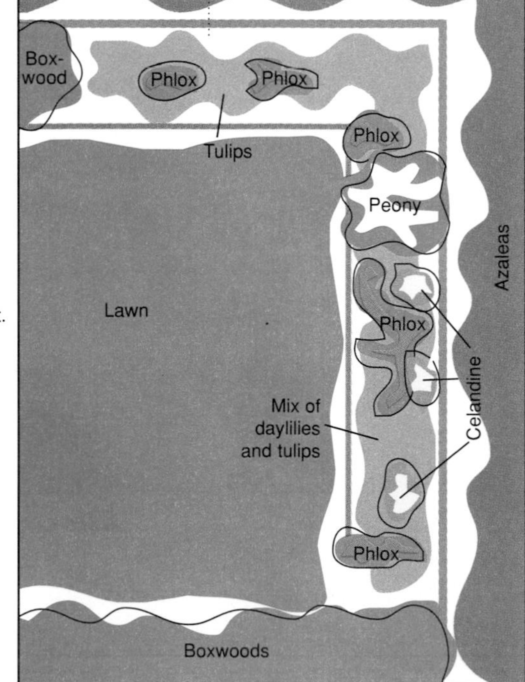

SHOWPLACE AREAS
Lawns and Borders

Q: I agreed to put on a garden party to raise funds for a local charity. It's nearly Christmas now, and the event is the first of June. What can I do in the next six months to make sure the garden looks beautiful for the party?

A: There needs to be plenty of lawn area for tables and chairs, and the lawn must be tough enough to take the traffic of many people walking on it. Try a bluegrass mixture in Region A, a tall fescue in Region B, and a St. Augustinegrass in Region C. It's best to put your flowers in a border at the outer edges of the lawn, so guests don't trip over flower beds.

For a beautiful, instant lawn, you'd be smart to lay down sod. Be sure to tell your sod installer that you need a grass variety that will tolerate heavy traffic, and that it must be fully established by the middle of May.

Annuals are the best choice for the flower borders, because they tend to grow faster, have more flowers, and bloom longer than most perennials. For shady areas, some good choices are white wax begonia, blue ageratum, and pink impatiens. For sunny areas, try white feverfew, red and yellow zinnia, yellow marigold, and golden calendula. Hostas are perennials, but they come on very fast with their dramatic foliage and so would be an effective contrast to all the bright flowers.

Plant the seedlings in time for them to be in glorious bloom for your party.

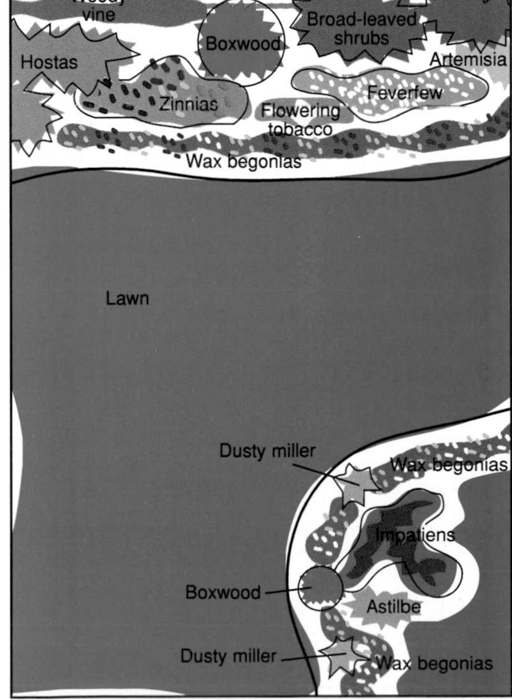

WHAT YOU NEED:

REGION

Plants for Regions A, B, & C

- **6 Hostas**
- **5 Zinnias**
- **20 Wax begonias**
- **5 Feverfew**
- **12 Impatiens**
- **1 Astilbe**
- **2 Dusty millers**
- **6 Flowering tobacco**
- **3 Boxwoods**
- **1 Artemisia**

No alternative plants are recommended. For suggested lawn care products, *see page 113.*

Q: Our front yard was completely destroyed by spring floods last year. Nothing is left except a few trees. Since I have to start from scratch with new landscaping, I've decided I want the yard to be a showplace garden. I'd like it to be serene and quiet with lots of flowers, a place to stroll. How do I begin?

A: Find a ball of white string and a handful of old-fashioned hairpins. Lay the string on the ground in the shape you want for the borders, and pin it in place with the hairpins. Move the string around until you have the shapes and curves you like best.

Be sure to leave space for a nice wide path (the traditional standard is wide enough for two people to walk comfortably together); figure 3 to 4 feet wide. Use grass for the paths; it's pleasantly soft underfoot and quiet to walk on. A good selection would be Scotts® Shady for Region A or Tri-Blend fescue for Region B.

Mixed perennial and annual borders will give the showplace effect you're after. Use annuals to provide color until the perennials fill in and, in later years, to give a summer show after the spring-blooming perennials have flowered. Select perennials that will flourish in the dappled shade of the trees. Some possibilities include azalea, rhododendron, helleborus, astilbe, columbine, Japanese anemone, fern, hosta, violet, and variegated goutweed (a groundcover). Attractive shade-loving annuals are impatiens, forget-me-not, and pansy. Add in flowering shrubs in the background to increase the sense of quiet enclosure and peacefulness.

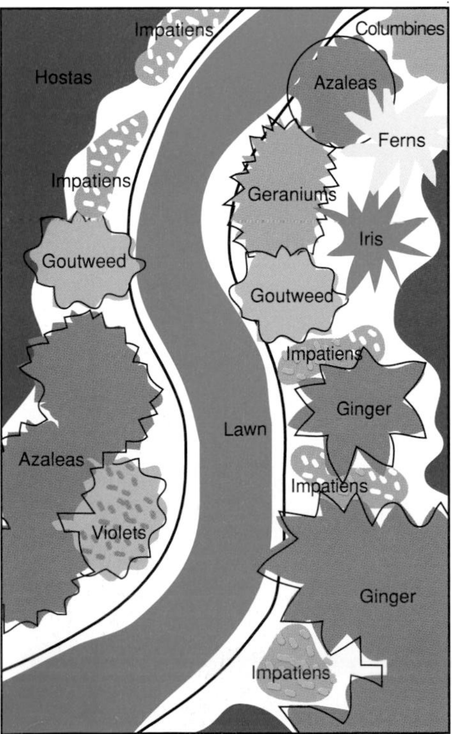

WHAT YOU NEED:

Plants for Region B

- **6 Impatiens**
- **4 Hostas**
- **4 Azaleas**
- **3 Columbines**
- **6 Goutweed**
- **4 Violets**
- **6 Ginger**
- **3 Geraniums**
- **1 Iris**
- **3 Ferns**

Regional plant alternatives listed on pages 120-123. For suggested lawn care products, see page 113.

8 SHOWPLACE AREAS
Garden Paths

Q: After years of plotting and planning, my garden looks great. However, I've tried several kinds of paths—gravel, logs, stepping-stones—but they always end up awash in mud, thanks to spring rains. What kind of path will let me enjoy my garden without having to wear rubber boots to my knees?

A: Clear out whatever was the last incarnation of the pathway and put in a grass path. If you're in a cold climate, look for a seed mixture specifically formulated for hard-use areas, such as Scotts® Play®, a mixture of perennial ryegrass and Kentucky bluegrass varieties. It germinates quickly and gives a fine-textured, durable lawn that resists weeds.

If you're in Region B, consider using Scotts Classic Estates®, a blend of seeds of drought-resistant, dark-green fescues. If you prefer to plug or sod, try a zoysia cultivar. Whichever grass you choose, you should be able to spend most of your time admiring your lovely garden instead of cleaning mud off your boots.

WHAT YOU NEED:

REGION

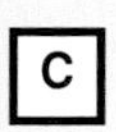

Plants for Regions A & B

- **1 Dogwood**
- **10 Azaleas**
- **40 Tulips**
- **25 Forget-me-nots**

Regional plant alternatives listed on pages 120-123. For suggested lawn care products, see page 113.

15 ft.

21 ft.

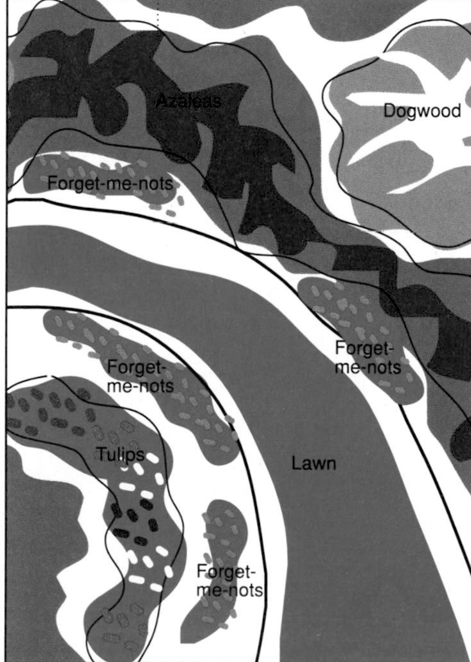

9 **SHOWPLACE AREAS**
Garden Paths

Q: Our back yard is enclosed by shrubbery except for a battered wooden gate with a cracked concrete pad in front. We'd like a more attractive entrance to the yard, but aren't sure how to go about it, especially since we don't want to damage the lawn or any of the existing plants. Any suggestions?

A: Remove the gate, gateposts, and concrete pad. Replace the concrete with a narrow brick entry. Replace the gate with a rose arch. Plant the rose arch with a climbing rose on one side. On the other side, put in an evergreen vine, such as morning glory, bower vine, or violet trumpet vine. This gives you two shows of flowers, and the evergreen vine will cover the bare rose canes in the winter.

On either side of the arch, put in mirror borders alongside the brick. Mirror borders are almost identical as they face each other. Use heartleaf bergenia for its bold leaves, Serbian bellflower for its masses of blue flowers, and giant foxglove next to the arch to emphasize the vertical lines of the arch.

With only a half-dozen or so different plants, your entry will have taken on both charm and grace, enticing the eye and framing the expanse of beautiful green lawn in flowers.

WHAT YOU NEED:

REGION

Plants for Regions A & B

- **2 Climbing roses**
- **1 Hosta**
- **12 Serbian bellflowers**
- **6 Bergenia**
- **3 Foxglove**

Regional plant alternatives listed on pages 120-123. For suggested lawn care products, see page 113.

14 ft.

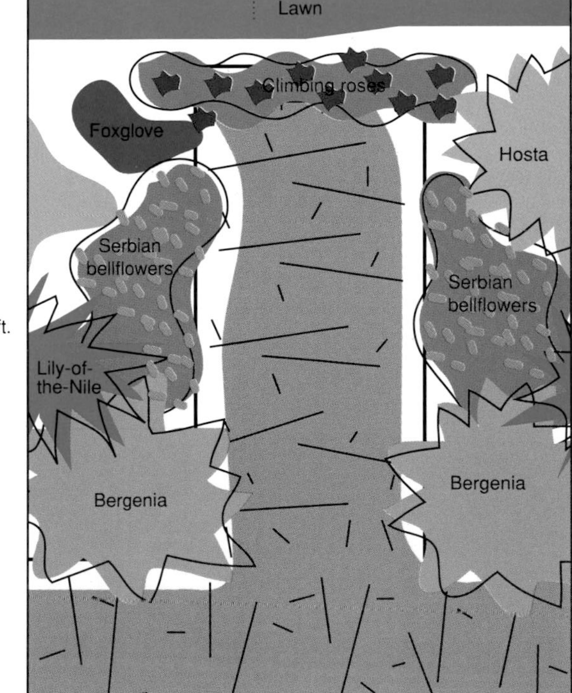

18 ft.

SHOWPLACE AREAS
Garden Paths

Q: Our back yard is a woodland garden with an alley of shade-loving plants. A wide, irregularly shaped path winds from the house through the trees. Flagstone or brick is too expensive, and concrete would ruin the effect, but the dirt path with dead leaves doesn't enhance the garden either. What should we do?

A: Grass works well with the woodland look, adapts well to irregular shapes, is soft and quiet underfoot, and is far less expensive to put in than paving materials, such as brick or stone.

If you're in Region A and the path gets only light summer use, think about putting in a grass path seeded with Scotts® Shady grass seed mixture of premium fescues, Kentucky bluegrass, and perennial ryegrass. If the path gets regular use, Scotts Family® grass-seed mixture is an excellent all-purpose blend that takes moderate traffic well.

In Region B, consider using Scotts Mirage, a blend of drought-resistant, low-growing fescues. Bermudagrass cultivars are not for pathways, because they tend to stray into flower beds and borders.

WHAT YOU NEED:

REGION

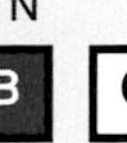

A B C

Plants for Regions A & B

3 Dogwoods
7 Azaleas
15 Primroses
100 Forget-me-nots

Regional plant alternatives listed on pages 120-123. For suggested lawn care products, see page 113.

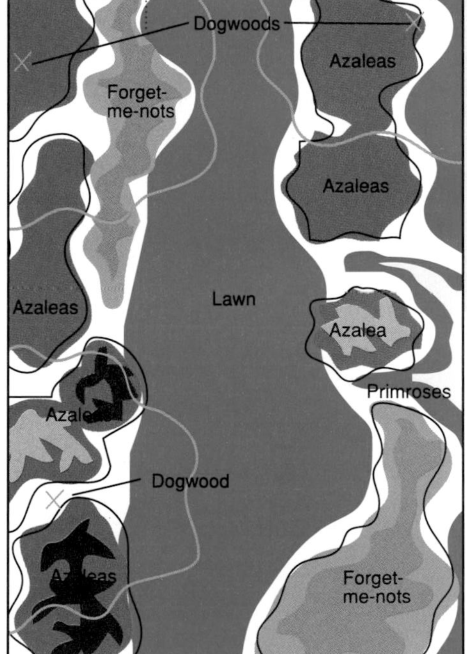

11 SHOWPLACE AREAS
Fancy Shapes

Q: I love my lawn and borders, but the yard's straight edges are boring. I'd like to do something creative and unexpected with the lawn itself. Any ideas?

A: Consider planting the flowers in a border around a fancy shape, such as a heart-shaped lawn. Mark out the size and shape of heart you want with string. Plant the borders after the unneeded lawn area is removed. Be sure to leave a break in the flower border to provide access for mowing the lawn. Use a kneeling pad or a piece of plywood to work on so the grass doesn't get damaged while you're planting. Some fast-growing annuals include petunia, dusty miller, French marigold, and dwarf dahlia. A climbing rose would be attractive growing on the fence. Think about planting climbing 'Cécile Brünner,' often called the "sweetheart rose," to stay with the heart theme.

To keep the focus of the garden where it belongs, plant the opposite side of any paths you might have in low-key, low-maintenance groundcovers. A very pretty, simple effect can be achieved with a standard wisteria (a wisteria vine grown on a single trunk to look like a small tree) planted in the middle, surrounded by a patch of variegated goutweed *(Aegopodium)* and bordered by ajuga.

WHAT YOU NEED:

REGION

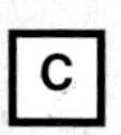

Plants for Regions A & B

- 12 Petunias
- 18 French marigolds
- 10 Ajuga
- 3 Pinks (dianthus)
- 1 Dahlia
- 6 Dusty millers
- 1 Juniper
- 1 Weeping juniper
- 2 Climbing roses
- 8 Black-eyed Susans

Regional plant alternatives listed on pages 120-123. For suggested lawn care products, see page 113.

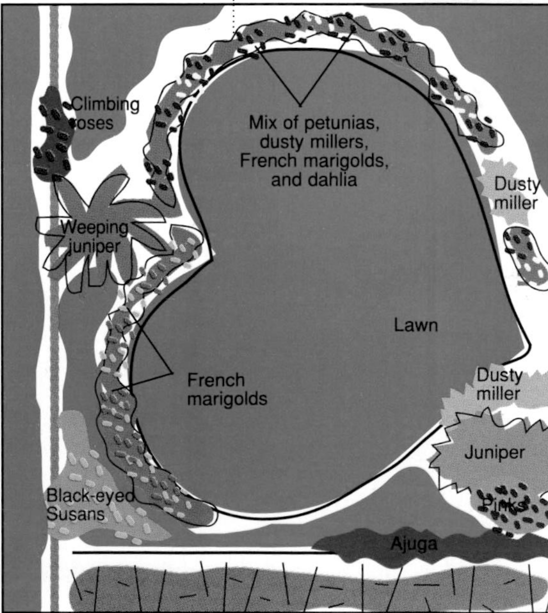

12 SHOWPLACE AREAS
Fancy Shapes

Q: I'm a serious bird-watcher. We have a large yard that is mostly lawn, but some of the lawn is in dense shade from the surrounding trees, which makes it patchy, sparse, and hard to mow. I'd like to address that problem, attract more birds, and do something special with my lawn. Can I do all three?

A: Solve two of your problems at once by taking out the lawn area that's hard to mow and replacing it with an attractive stepping-stone path. It'll give you a place to stand while looking at birds.

You'll need three things to attract birds: food, water, and cover. Create an island bed in the center of the lawn with shrubs and evergreens. Choose plants that have berries or fruit to provide food. Some shrubs that qualify include pyracantha, hawthorn, cotoneaster, and holly. Many evergreens produce cones that contain seeds that birds eat. Supply water with an attractive birdbath. The surrounding trees provide plenty of safe cover, well out of the reach of cats and other predators.

The island bed also serves several purposes: It reduces the amount of lawn to mow, supplants the patchy grass with shrubs, and offers birds exactly what they need to make your yard a feeding and resting stop on the migratory route as well as a place to nest in the breeding season.

WHAT YOU NEED:

REGION

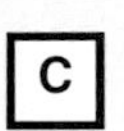

Plants for Region B

- **1 Colorado spruce**
- **1 Colorado blue spruce**
- **9 Mexican daisies**
- **14 Campanula**
- **2 Artemisia**
- **4 Salvia**

Regional plant alternatives listed on pages 120-123. For suggested lawn care products, see page 113.

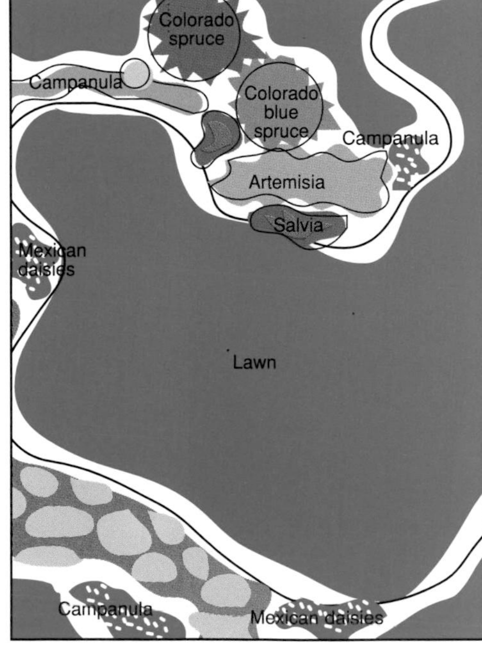

SHOWPLACE AREAS
Fancy Shapes

Q: Our condominium complex recently built broad, well-lighted brick paths. Now no one in the homeowners' association can agree on how we should landscape the sides of the paths. Some people want lawn, some want flowers, and others want shrubs. What can we do to satisfy everyone?

WHAT YOU NEED:

REGION

Plants for Regions A, B, & C

100 Wax begonias
12 Dogwoods
18 Spirea
1 Serviceberry

Regional plant alternatives listed on pages120-123. For suggested lawn care products, see page 113.

A: Put in grass directly alongside the paths. It softens the effect of the brick. Lay out the lawn in a broad swath that follows the graceful curves of the paths. A good choice for Region A is Scotts® Picture® ryegrass/bluegrass mix. Good choices for Region B are zoysiagrasses or Sonesta Bermudagrass. (If you use the bermudagrass, put in bender board along the edges of the shrub and flower borders to keep them where they belong.) If you are located in Region C, try St. Augustinegrass.

In the hollows of some of the curves, both along the paths and along the lawn, mass some long-blooming annuals. It's important to choose flowers that have a neat habit, such as wax begonias, so they don't sprawl onto the path where they might get run over or walked on.

To soften the straight lines of the buildings, plant a shrub border with low-growing shrubs next to the lawn and taller shrubs next to the buildings. Dwarf evergreens would be a good choice for the low-growing shrubs. They provide attractive year-round color and require minimal maintenance. For the foundation shrubs, consider plants that offer multiple benefits: flowers, fragrance, variegated foliage, seasonal color, and/or winter berries. Possible candidates (depending on your climate) include mock orange, which has flowers, orange-blossom fragrance, and gray-green leaves edged in white; heavenly bamboo, which has pretty sprays of dainty white flowers, leaves that turn red but don't fall in autumn, and bright red winter berries; and holly, which has purple stems, winter berries, and spiny, glossy blue-green leaves.

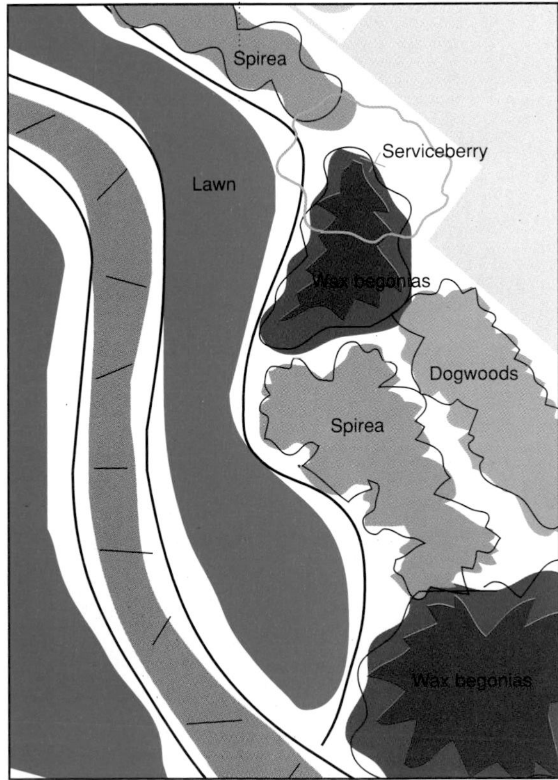

SHOWPLACE AREAS
Low Maintenance

Q: We have a large back yard that adjoins a small woods on our property. We need a clear transition from the lawn and flowers of the yard to the wooded area. There's already a stone path and a simple rail fence and gate. What else can we do to make the two areas distinct from each other?

A: Plant the sides of the path leading to the woods with hardy, shade-loving, low-maintenance groundcovers. A variety of groundcovers gives color contrast and textural interest. Plant a swath of pachysandra on one section of the stone path and a patch of ajuga (also called carpet bugle) on an adjoining section. The yellow-green foliage of pachysandra contrasts well with the spiky blue flowers and dark-green foliage of ajuga. On the opposite side of the path, plant another hardy, low-maintenance groundcover, such as English ivy, for another contrasting leaf shape, texture, and color.

Other than normal garden watering and fertilizing once or twice a year, the only care these groundcovers should require is an occasional trimming to keep them off the stone path.

WHAT YOU NEED:

REGION

Plants for Regions B & C

100 Pachysandra
75 Ajuga
24 English ivies

Regional plant alternatives listed on pages 120-123. For suggested fertilizers, see page 105.

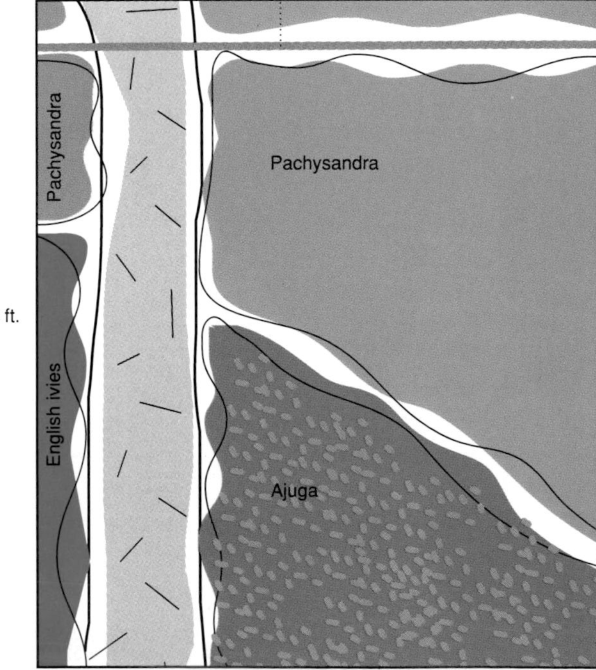

SHOWPLACE AREAS
Low Maintenance

Q: No matter what I do, people keep cutting across one section of the lawn. I've posted signs, reseeded, and enclosed the area with string on stakes, but nothing has worked. Is there a more practical option?

A: Since that area is clearly a good way to get from point A to point B, put in a path of stepping-stones and landscape both sides with low-maintenance groundcovers, shrubs, and flowers.

For a groundcover, consider ajuga. It spreads quickly and has the extra bonus of attractive blue flowers for several months of the year. An evergreen daylily in the midst of the ajuga gives good foliage contrast and a long season of bloom in the summer. Good, easy-care shrubs are Mexican orange, mock orange, and Indian hawthorn. All of these shrubs flower, and the blooms of both the Mexican orange and mock orange have a delightful orange-blossom fragrance.

WHAT YOU NEED:

REGION

A B C

Plants for Region C

- **1 Mexican orange**
- **5 Indian hawthorns**
- **2 Daylilies**
- **3 Mock oranges**
- **60 Ajuga**

Regional plant alternatives listed on pages 120-123. For suggested fertilizers, see page 105.

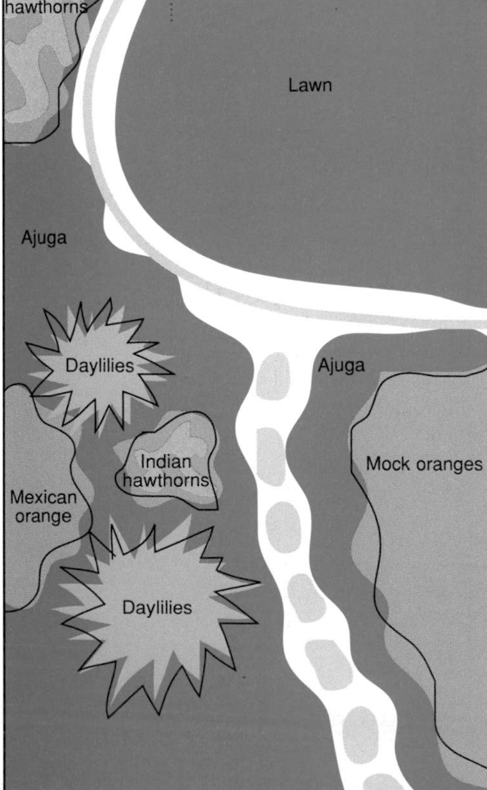

YARD SIZE
Small Space

Q: I live alone in a small house with an even smaller yard. I should probably just pave it and call it a patio, but I'd really love to have some flowers and a grassy place where I could sunbathe now and then. Is there an answer besides concrete?

A: The great thing about small spaces is that they don't require much to make a big difference. Here you can accomplish two things at once by going for the bold effect. Plant large flowering shrubs like rhododendrons, and you achieve privacy from the neighbors and colorful flowers, all in one fell swoop. In front of the shrubs on one side, mass big yellow tulips for a bright spot of spring color. Overplant them later with long-blooming summer annuals—perhaps some red-and-white-striped petunias.

Fill the space in the middle with a nice, soft lawn, perfect for walking on barefoot and taking in the sun. Treat yourself to an instant lawn by laying down sod. Ordinarily, laying sod is the most expensive method of putting in a new lawn, but, here again, having a small space works to your advantage; it's a lot less costly to put in a little lawn than a big one. If you want to save money, you can seed the lawn. In Region A, look for a sun-loving Kentucky bluegrass mixture. In Region B, a tall fescue works well, and in Region C, choose a bermudagrass.

For the price of a few big shrubs, 30 tulips, and a bit of sod, you'll have a delightful little garden, exactly right for relaxing.

WHAT YOU NEED:

REGION

Plants for Regions A, B, & C

5 Rhododendrons
30 Tulips

Regional plant alternatives listed on pages 120-123. For suggested lawn care products, see page 113.

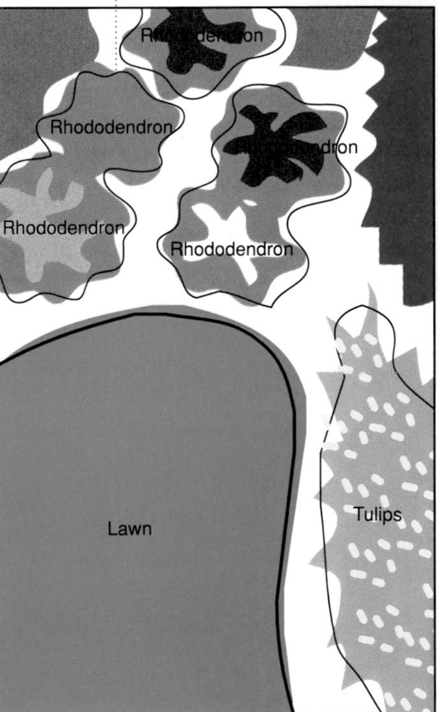

YARD SIZE
Small Space

Q: I've just purchased a turn-of-the-century Victorian house in the heart of the city. The yard is small, but it appears that it may once have had a wonderful garden. Unfortunately, time and neglect have taken a terrible toll. What can I do to restore it to its former splendor?

A: Create wide flower borders on each side of the yard. Prepare the borders by turning the soil 2 feet deep and digging in plenty of rich topsoil and organic matter. Fill the borders with easy-to-grow, sun-loving flowers, such as calendula, blanket flower, coreopsis, or Canterbury bells. Edge the borders with low-growing annuals, such as sweet alyssum and pansies.

Fill in the central space of the yard with a formal, shaped lawn. A good choice for a sunny situation in Region C is Scotts® Sonesta Bermudagrass. Once the lawn is established, fertilize it on a regular schedule to keep it in display condition all year round. Since the Victorians appreciated rather formal elements, cut spaces out of the lawn area, and plant clipped boxwood balls.

Large pots of azaleas will help make the space feel larger when the flowers are in bloom by drawing the eye the entire length of the garden. The straight lines of the flower borders and the lawn will make this small space feel formal and elegant. The rounded masses of color from the azaleas and flowers soften those lines to make the garden feel both charming and welcoming.

WHAT YOU NEED:

REGION

Plants for Region C

- **6 Azaleas**
- **10 Boxwoods**
- **24 Calendula**
- **4 English ivies**
- **20 Ajuga**
- **5 Canterbury bells**
- **10 Pansies**
- **8 Sweet alyssum**

Regional plant alternatives listed on pages 120-123. For suggested lawn care products, see page 113.

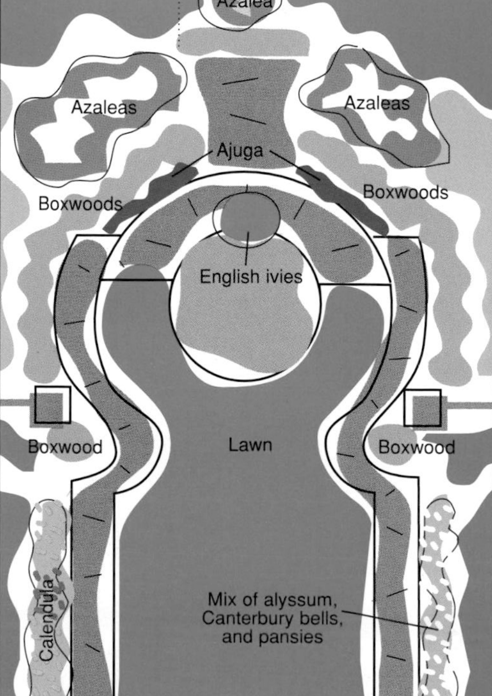

YARD SIZE
Small Space

Q: My back yard is a small, enclosed courtyard that's surrounded by two-story houses. This is a warm climate, and all that brick absorbs—and reflects—a lot of heat, despite the shade cast by the other houses. Is there any way to reduce the heat level and soften the visual effect of the brick paving and brick walls?

A: The most effective way to bring down the heat is to remove some of the paved area and replace it with grass. Make the lawn circular or oval; the curves will help relieve the hard-edged feeling of straight lines and right angles. Border the grass with brick that matches the walls to tie them together. In Region C, St. Augustinegrass may be your best choice simply because it tolerates shade so well, even dense shade. It can be sprigged or plugged and is fairly fast-growing.

Leave a border about 3 feet wide in front of the walls for flowers. Lots of spectacular flowers love the combination of dappled shade and mild climate, among them impatiens, poor man's rhododendron, poor man's orchid, fuchsia, wax begonia, and tuberous begonia. Lots of great-looking foliage plants like it, too, including coleus and fancy-leaved caladium.

Small, summer-flowering trees can enhance the garden as well, lowering the temperature with shade and lightening the garden with bright flowers. Crape myrtle does this beautifully.

WHAT YOU NEED:

REGION

 A  

Plants for Regions B & C

- **3 Crape myrtles**
- **16 Impatiens**
- **1 Honeysuckle vine**
- **5 Daylilies**
- **2 Yews**
- **2 Scotch broom**

Regional plant alternatives listed on pages 120-123. For suggested lawn care products, see page 113.

24 ft.

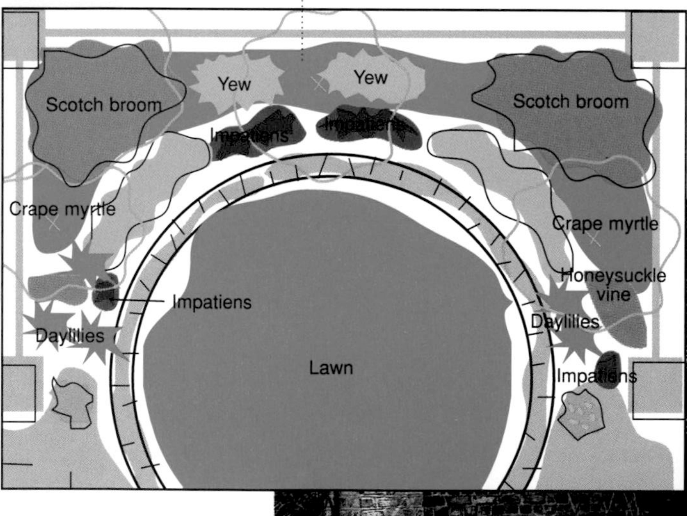

17 ft.

19

YARD SIZE
Small Space

WHAT YOU NEED:

REGION

Plants for Region C

55 Daylilies
16 Star jasmines

Regional plant alternatives listed on pages 120-123. For suggested lawn care products, see page 113.

Q: I'm a single parent, work full time, and feel as though I need to spend whatever spare time I have with my kids. On the other hand, I would like a few easy-care flowers while maintaining our back yard as a place for kids to play. Is there a way to have a nice yard without driving myself to exhaustion?

A: A lawn is the perfect place for children to play. They can do somersaults or learn to stand on their heads without hurting themselves, and they can run barefoot through the sprinklers when it's hot. Involve them in the process of seeding a new lawn, and you may find yourself with some small gardeners on your hands. For a durable, hard-use lawn, choose Scotts® Play® mixture. It's fine-textured, which means it feels nice on little feet, and it resists weeds, which means it takes less work to keep it looking good.

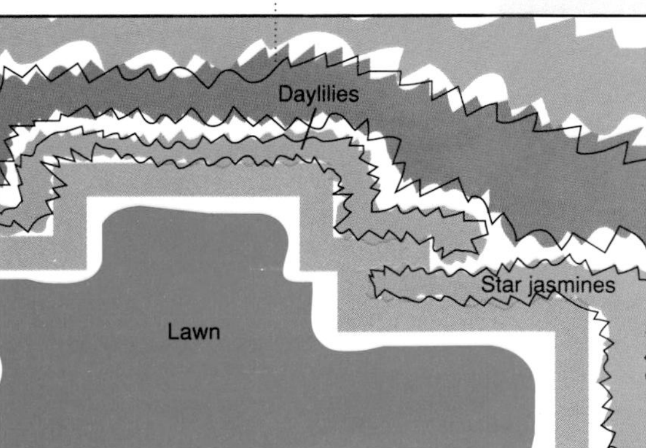

Raised-bed benches will provide you with easily worked flower beds and a place to sit—while keeping the kids out of them. Fill the beds with tough, easy-to-grow shrubs and flowers. Excellent choices for flowers in a warm climate include evergreen daylily, ivy geranium, and star jasmine. The star jasmine has the advantage of being magnificently fragrant as well. For large shrubs, ceanothus, glossy abelia, and the pale pink *Lavatera* 'Barnsley' are all handsome and drought-resistant once established; the lavatera is also extremely fast-growing.

Once the initial planting is done, you can pretty much just watch the garden grow. The chores consist of turning on the sprinklers, mowing the little lawn, and feeding everything twice a year.

YARD SIZE
Large Space

Q: When our children were growing up, we used our back lawn as their play area. Now that the children are grown and gone, we'd like to have a little less lawn to mow. What are some attractive alternatives?

A: Set off the lawn with wide borders of a low-maintenance groundcover, such as English ivy. Lay bricks flat along the edges of the lawn to accomplish three purposes: a handsome edging, a good mowing strip for easier mowing, and a barrier to keep both the ivy and the lawn where they belong.

Build a long, low, raised brick bed and, before planting, amend the soil with organic matter, such as Scotts® 3-in-1 Organic Mix. Fill the flower bed with easy-to-grow, sun-loving perennials, such as daylily, summer lily, bee balm, and purple loosestrife.

To put the lawn in prime condition, follow a four-application lawn program, such as the Scotts Turf Builder® Annual Program (see page 111).

WHAT YOU NEED:

REGION

   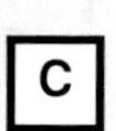

Plants for Regions A & B

- **8 Columbines**
- **3 Bee balm**
- **4 Loosestrife**
- **4 Lilies**
- **8 Daylilies**
- **360 English ivies**
- **12 Lamb's ears**

Regional plant alternatives listed on pages 120-123. For suggested lawn care products, see page 113.

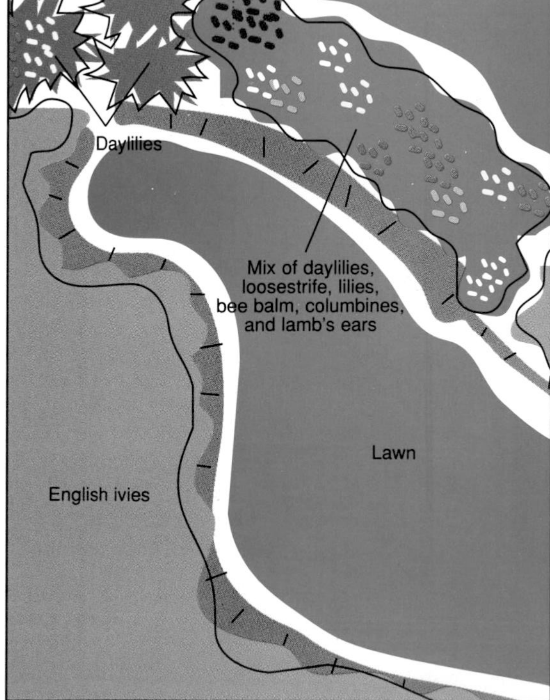

21 YARD SIZE
Large Space

Q: Now that our yew hedge is fully grown in, I'd like to use it as a background for a large English perennial border. As it is, the lawn grows to the base of the hedge, and there's a paved walk that borders the lawn. How do I shape the new border?

A: The rule of thumb in garden design is that straight lines are formal, curves are informal. Since the yew hedge and the paved walk are both made up of straight lines and right angles, perhaps it would be a good idea to balance the look with some wide, sweeping curves.

Take a long garden hose and place one end at the corner of the path. Stretch it out to the far end of the hedge. Then pull it into the curves you find appealing. Once you've found a shape you like, mark the line with metal garden stakes and white string.

Remove the grass and amend the soil of the new flower bed with rich topsoil and organic material. Some classic flowers for an English perennial border are blue false indigo, gas plant, variegated iris, hardy geranium, heartleaf bergenia, and catmint. On the other side of the path, put in a bed of Welsh poppies for additional color.

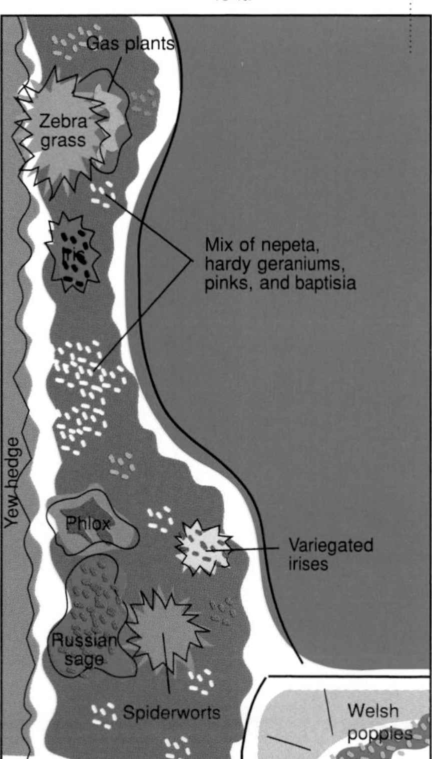

WHAT YOU NEED:

Plants for Region B

- 3 Baptisia
- 3 Nepeta
- 2 Variegated irises
- 2 Gas plants
- 3 Hardy geraniums
- 20 Welsh poppies
- 4 Irises
- 2 Spiderworts
- 6 Pinks (dianthus)
- 3 Phlox
- 1 Yew hedge
- 1 Russian sage
- 1 Zebra grass

Regional plant alternatives listed on pages 120-123. For suggested lawn care products, see page 113.

Q: A new house is being built on the lot next door, and suddenly our large back yard doesn't feel very private any more. Is there anything we can do with landscaping to regain a sense of privacy?

A: Put in a large shrubbery border along the property line to keep your lawn private.

Fill the area with substantial shrubs, such as rhododendrons, dwarf conifers, and Japanese maples. Dwarf conifers are extremely dense, blocking not only the sight line but absorbing a great deal of sound as well. Rhododendrons are green year-round and bloom spectacularly in the spring. Some rhododendron hybrids, such as 'My Lady' and 'Mi Amor,' have fragrant flowers; others, such as PJM, have fragrant foliage. By choosing individual plants carefully, you can block out the neighboring property and have flowers and fragrance as well. Japanese maples put on a three-season show; they have pale-pink or lime-green new growth in spring, dainty foliage in the summer, and brilliant color in the fall.

WHAT YOU NEED:

Plants for Region B

- 2 **Japanese maples**
- 2 **Rhododendrons**
- 11 **Dwarf conifers**

Regional plant alternatives listed on pages 120-123. For suggested lawn care products, see page 113.

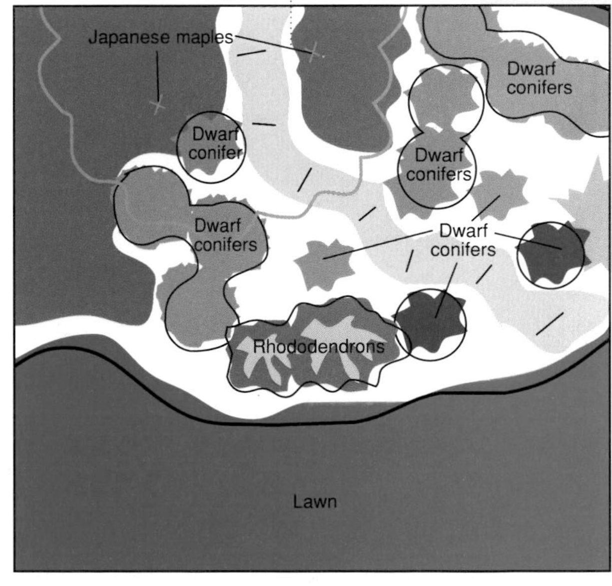

23 YARD SIZE
Large Space

Q: After a month spent in England, I want a garden that has that established-for-centuries look the British do so well. I don't have acres to work with, but I do have a big lawn dotted with mature trees. How can I make it look as though there should be an English country manor somewhere nearby?

A: What the British do better than just about anybody else is grow magnificent lawns. The key to a great lawn in this country is a four-application program (see page 111). An annual program feeds your lawn and keeps pests and diseases out.

Under any deciduous trees at the far end of your yard, carve out a couple of large sections for flowering-shrub borders. Leave a grassy path between them to stroll down at leisure (and to work from when you're planting). Amend the new planting areas heavily with Scotts® Tree & Shrub Planting Soil. Fill the borders with camellias for winter bloom and azaleas for spring bloom. Include a small flowering tree, such as star magnolia. Mulch both borders.

WHAT YOU NEED:

REGION

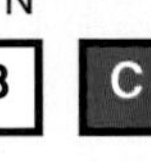

Plants for Region C

- **2 Magnolias**
- **6 Camellias**
- **8 Azaleas**

Regional plant alternatives listed on pages 120-123. For suggested lawn care products, see page 113.

55 ft.

87 ft.

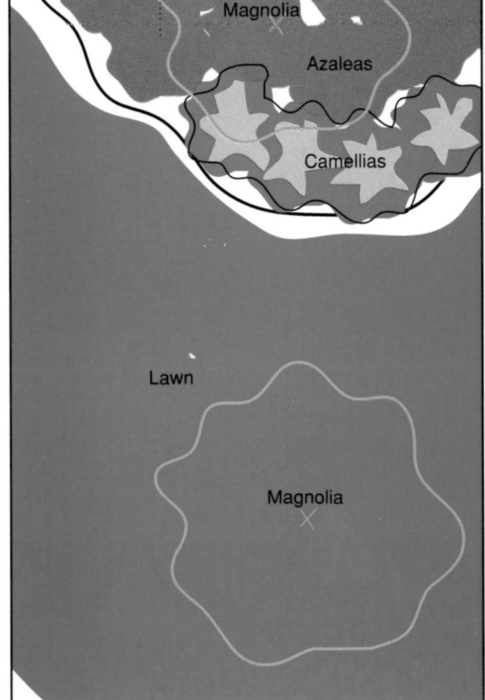

24 **YARD SIZE**
Large Space

Q: **We just bought a weekend house in the country with an enormous lot. The back yard is nothing but badly neglected lawn that stretches from the house to a belt of trees at the far end of the property. I'd like to add some interest to the expanse, but whatever I plant needs to be self-reliant. Any suggestions?**

WHAT YOU NEED:

REGION

Plants for Regions A, B, & C

- **40 Sedum (three varieties)**
- **6 Daisies**
- **20 Ornamental grasses**
- **3 Violas**
- **12 Pinks (dianthus)**

Regional plant alternatives listed on pages 120-123. For suggested lawn care products, see page 113.

A: To make the lawn a showpiece in itself, renovate any bare places with Scotts® PatchMaster®, a complete package of grass seed, fertilizer, and mulch.

To create interest, add some border areas and some island beds. In addition to being eye-catching, they also cut down on the amount of lawn you have to mow. Large, sculptural rocks add visual interest and textural contrast to the smooth lawn. Put them in the borders, and plant flowers or groundcovers around them. Mulch the beds.

Ornamental grasses in the island beds bring a whole new element to the landscape as they bend with every breeze. Not only are they unusual and lovely, but the movement is attractive as well.

Good choices for ornamental grasses include green-and-white-striped ribbon grass, tall cordgrass, tasseled fountain grass, and the bluish sheep fescue. Blue fescue is a small beauty with needle-thin, blue-grey clusters. If it is planted in bouquet-size mounds in geometric patterns, it is a wonderful choice for a formal garden.

A good foil to the spiky green grasses would be sedum, viola, pinks, and Shasta daisy. 'Autumn Joy' sedum has soft grey-green leaves and blooms in late fall with bright pink flowers; Shasta daisy blooms with bright white and yellow flowers; pinks bloom in many vivid shades of pink; and viola adds a touch of purple.

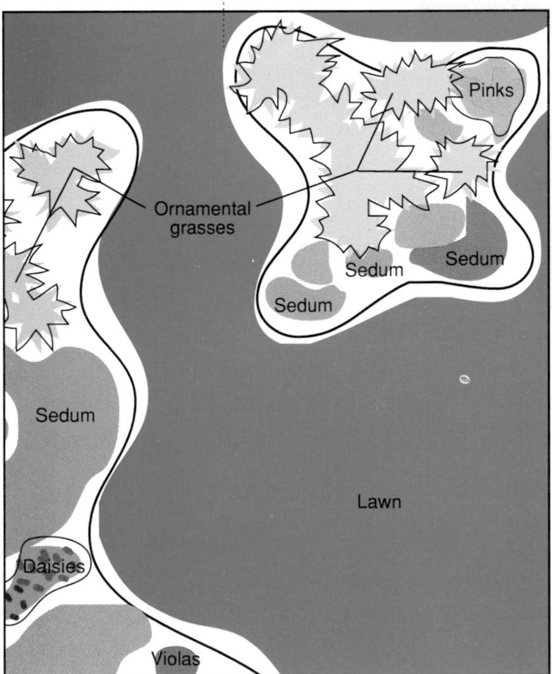

YARD SIZE
Large Space

Q: We have a large, level back yard that is mostly lawn. My elderly mother has recently come to live with us, and I'd like to have a portion of the lawn made into a quiet little nook where she can sit in the sunshine. How can we make her a pleasant, sunny space all her own?

A: Take a corner of the lawn and create a sense of enclosure by surrounding it with shrubs and ornamental grasses. Shrubs contribute mass and density; ornamental grasses create textural contrast and movement. The two work well together.

Lay out the size and shape of each border using stakes and white string. Be sure to make the borders wide enough to allow for plenty of growing room; shrubs need space to spread. Remove the lawn and prepare the soil by digging it 2 feet down and amending it with organic material. Scotts® planting soils are a rich mix of organic materials premixed for your convenience.

Fill the background with large rounded shrubs, such as winged euonymus, and light, airy ornamental grasses, such as Chinese silver grass, ribbon grass, or crimson fountain grass.

Edge the borders with bunches of low-growing perennials, such as silver-foliaged artemisia and cranesbill geraniums, for color and textural contrast.

Add a handsome wooden bench, and your mother will have a pretty, comfortable place to sit and enjoy the sunshine.

WHAT YOU NEED:

REGION

Plants for Regions A & B

15 Cranesbill geraniums
4 Ribbon grasses
4 Miscanthus
3 Artemisia
2 Winged euonymus

Regional plant alternatives listed on pages 120-123. For suggested lawn care products, see page 113.

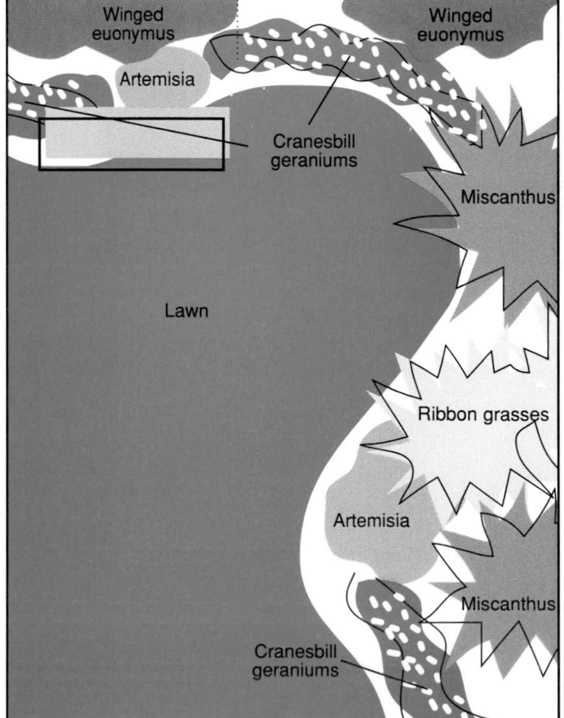

YARD SIZE
Large Space

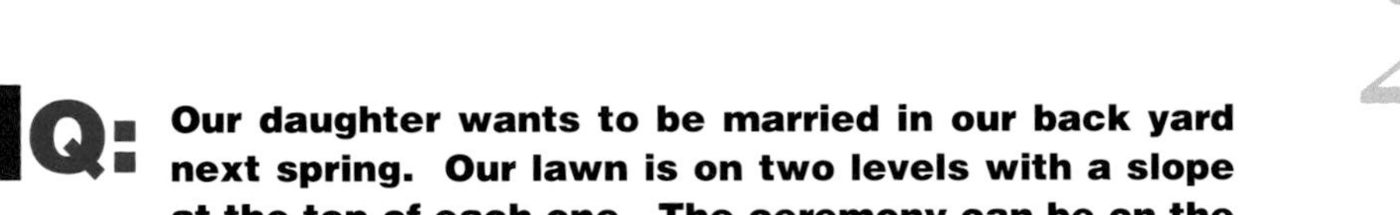

Q: Our daughter wants to be married in our back yard next spring. Our lawn is on two levels with a slope at the top of each one. The ceremony can be on the upper level under our dogwoods, and we can set up tables for the reception on the lower level. What can be done to make the sloped portions look attractive?

A: Use groundcovers to set the two levels off from each other, making them clearly distinct and separate. Groundcovers also provide flowers and an appealing textural contrast to the lawn.

On the intermediary slopes, plant large beds of blue-flowered periwinkle. Intermix yellow-flowering evergreen daylilies. Both of these plants are tough, drought tolerant, easy to grow, and easy to maintain. When they bloom, the blue and yellow will be an attractive color combination.

Plant English ivy on the slopes adjacent to the house. Like the periwinkle, it is an undemanding plant, capable of looking handsome without a lot of fussing.

WHAT YOU NEED:

REGION

Plants for Region B

2 Dogwoods
250 English ivies
40 Daylilies
200 Periwinkles

Regional plant alternatives listed on pages 120-123. For suggested lawn care products, see page 113.

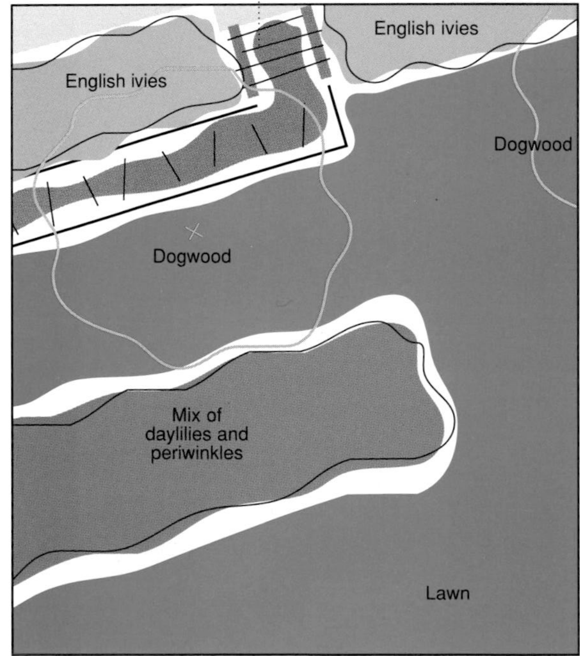

27 YARD SIZE
Large Space

Q: Our large lawn always has been my husband's pride and joy, but now that we're both retiring he says he'd like to have less lawn to mow. I'd love to have some roses and space for flowers, but I don't kneel and bend as well as I used to. Any ideas?

WHAT YOU NEED:

REGION

Plants for Regions B & C

- **2 Climbing roses**
- **2 Roses**
- **1 New Zealand flax**

Regional plant alternatives listed on pages 120-123. For suggested lawn care products, see page 113.

A: Take some of that large lawn and turn it into a raised-bed garden. Along one side of the lawn, build double-decker raised beds 3 feet high, and fill them with good topsoil. With raised beds, you can plant all the flowers you want without bending at all; with a depth of 3 feet, you can plant almost anything—flowers, shrubs, or even small trees—because there's plenty of root room.

Consider putting in small Japanese maples for their delicate airy summer foliage and brilliant fall color. Plant a dwarf citrus tree or two for their flowers, fragrance, and fruit. Add some flowering shrubs, such as natal plum, veronica, heavenly bamboo, and mock orange. The plums and mock orange have powerfully fragrant white flowers; the veronica is covered with spikes of lavender flowers in late summer and early autumn; and the heavenly bamboo provides airy sprays of white flowers in spring, excellent foliage color in autumn, and bright red berries in winter. Fill in around the shrubs with undemanding, sun-loving perennials, such as lily-of-the-Nile, evergreen daylily, bearded iris, and fortnight lily.

And, of course, plant roses. Because roses are perennials, you can get them all planted in one short session, which shouldn't require too much kneeling and bending.

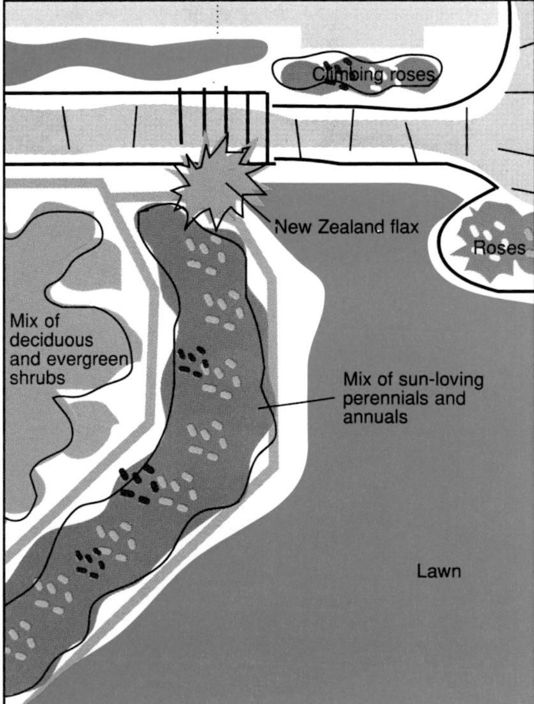

SPECIAL CONDITIONS
Gentle Slope

Q: Because our lot slopes gently, drainage isn't a problem. However, finding a groundcover that will take the slope, dense shade, and foot traffic is. What can we put in that will look good in our woodland garden even when walked on?

A: There aren't many groundcovers that will take foot traffic, and those that do, such as creeping thyme or Corsican mint, are typically used on a very small scale (for example, between steppingstones). The best green solution for foot traffic is grass, and the best solution for a gentle slope is gentle leveling.

Stay in keeping with the woodland look of your garden by putting in log risers wherever needed. Then level the soil behind them to create a series of wide steps. In Region A, use Scotts® Shady grass mixture, which is great for colder climates. Scotts Classic Estates® is an excellent choice for Region B, and in Region C plant St. Augustinegrass—a great choice for warm climates.

WHAT YOU NEED:

REGION

Plants for Regions A, B, & C

- **2 Junipers**
- **7 Azaleas**
- **2 Rhododendrons**
- **3 Weeping hemlocks**

Regional plant alternatives listed on pages 120-123. For suggested lawn care products, see page 113.

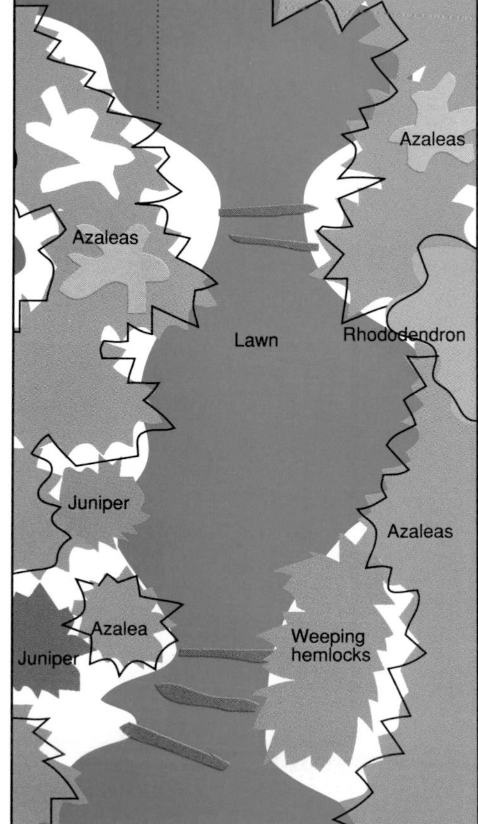

SPECIAL CONDITIONS
Gentle Slope

Q: Part of the hillside behind our house is gently sloped; other parts are fairly steep. We need to prevent erosion from heavy winter rains, and we'd like it to look attractive, too. What should we do?

A: Plant the steepest slopes with trailing gazania, a perennial groundcover that spreads rapidly and is particularly useful on banks. It blooms spectacularly in late spring with flowers so thick they form a solid sheet of color. It continues to bloom off and on throughout the year.

Seed the gentler slopes with bermudagrass, such as Scotts® Sonesta. It establishes quickly, is a good-looking, dark green color, and requires less watering and mowing than other turf grasses. Use bender board between the gazania and the bermudagrass to prevent them from straying into each other's territory.

Plant a pair of dwarf lemon trees at the top of the slopes; the yellow fruit echoes the yellow flowers of the gazanias. Plant a Hollywood juniper between the gazania beds to provide a strong contrast to the silvery leaves of the gazania and offer a striking silhouette as well.

WHAT YOU NEED:

REGION

Plants for Region C

- **250 Trailing gazanias**
- **2 Roses**
- **2 Dwarf citrus trees**
- **1 Bougainvillea**
- **1 Hollywood juniper**

Regional plant alternatives listed on pages 120-123. For suggested lawn care products, see page 113.

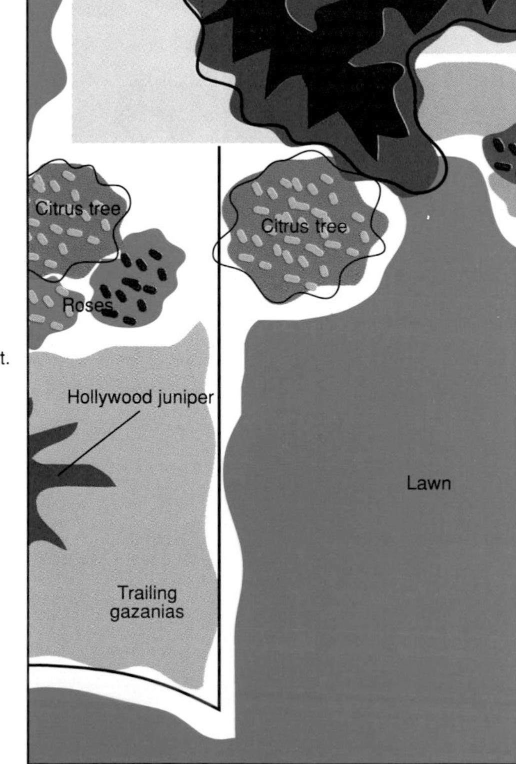

30

SPECIAL CONDITIONS
Steep Slope

Q: Our front lawn ends in a steep slope. It's hard to mow and hard to weed, and it always looks terrible. Surely there must be another way to deal with this bank. Do you have any ideas?

A: Cut off the lawn where the slope begins, leaving only the level area in grass. Amend the soil of the bank with a rich organic mix, such as one of the Scotts® planting soils. Cover the slope with plastic mulch cloth, securely pegged into place. The cloth will prevent both erosion and weeds. Make holes in the plastic wherever you need to plant, dig planting holes, and fertilize each hole. Choose groundcover plants whose roots help control erosion, such as low-maintenance creeping juniper and ajuga.

Stabilize the corners of the bank with large rocks, and plant strong foliage plants, such as lilyturf, astilbe (which blooms), juniper, and flowering rhododendron for good textural and color contrast.

Finish the bank off by covering the plastic with a mulch of bark chips for a neat, tidy appearance while the groundcovers fill in.

WHAT YOU NEED:

Plants for Region B

- 12 Rhododendrons
- 10 Creeping junipers
- 1 Maple tree
- 1 Ornamental grass
- 8 Pieris
- 5 Ajuga

Regional plant alternatives listed on pages 120-123. For suggested lawn care products, see page 113.

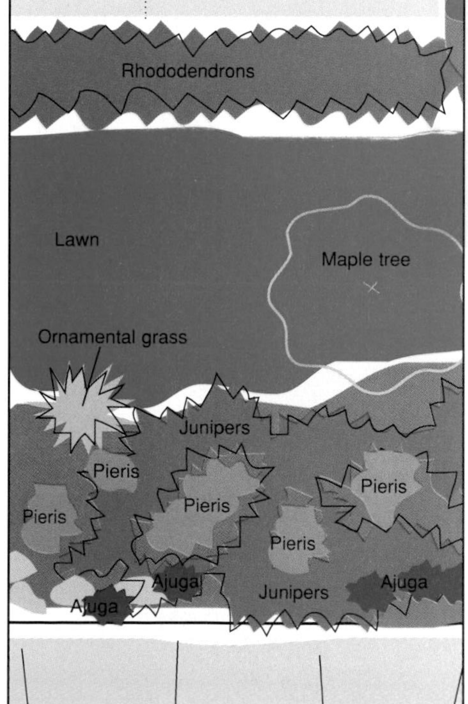

31 SPECIAL CONDITIONS
Steep Slope

Q: **We just cut down a dead tree on the slope behind our house. It's so steep that the surface vegetation was torn up in the process of hauling out the trunk and the branches. The slope is partially shaded in the summer by some mature maples. What can we plant to keep the winter rains from washing out the soil?**

A: Put in a hardy, fast-spreading groundcover, such as ajuga (carpet bugle). It spreads by runners to make a thick carpet of lustrous leaves and blooms from spring to early summer with showy spikes of dark blue flowers. There are a number of cultivars, some with dark green leaves, some with bronze or purplish leaves. In partial shade, the green-leaved ajugas look best (the purple-leaved and bronze-leaved types tend to lose their color unless they are in full sun). 'Jungle Green' and 'Giant Green' are two useful varieties; there is also a cultivar known as 'Variegata,' the leaves of which are edged and splotched with yellow. The fast, solid coverage of ajuga helps prevent soil erosion.

WHAT YOU NEED:

REGION

A

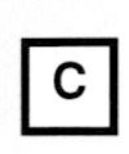

Plants for Region B

2 Maple trees
2000 Ajuga
3 Wisteria
2 Sword ferns

Regional plant alternatives listed on pages 120-123. For suggested fertilizers, see page 105.

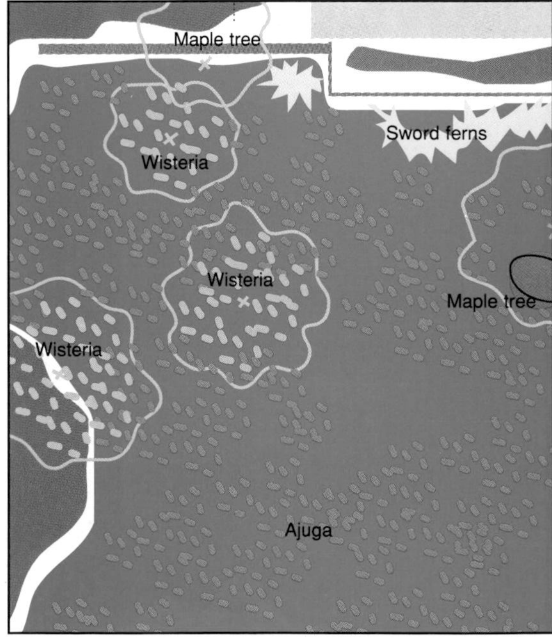

32 SPECIAL CONDITIONS
Steep Slope

Q: We live in a warm climate, and our house on the hill has a wonderful back view. Unfortunately, the view from the front is less wonderful—just a very steep slope down to the sidewalk. It does have a couple of retaining walls holding up the hillside. What can we can do to make the front yard more beautiful?

A: Fill that steep slope with sun-loving, drought-tolerant plants that love fast drainage and your warm climate. Some excellent choices are Lily-of-the-Nile, trailing lantana, bougainvillea, mock orange, evergreen daylily, bearded iris, butterfly iris, and fortnight lily.

To mask those concrete retaining walls, plant trailing rosemary just behind the edges of the walls and let it trail over them. In the narrow strip of soil between the sidewalk and the lower wall, tuck in society garlic.

To encourage faster growth, amend each planting hole with organic material, such as a rich Scotts® planting soil. A drip-irrigation system on an automatic timer will deliver water to each plant's roots without causing slope erosion.

Give the slope a season or two to fill in, and the view from the front will be as appealing as the view from the back.

WHAT YOU NEED:

REGION

Plants for Region C

- **6 Primrose jasmines**
- **3 Trailing lantanas**
- **6 Lily-of-the-Nile**
- **18 Mock oranges (*Pittosporum tobira*)**
- **12 Society garlic**
- **8 Trailing rosemary**

Regional plant alternatives listed on pages 120-123. For suggested fertilizers, see page 105.

30 ft.

44 ft.

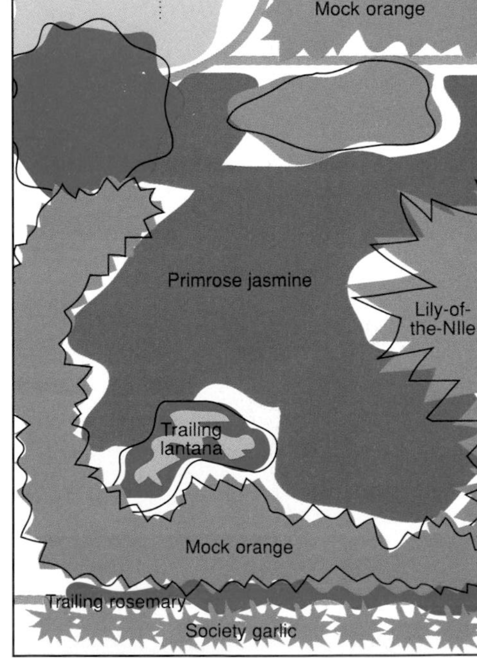

33

SPECIAL CONDITIONS
Steep Slope

Q: We have a huge lawn, and I love every square inch of it. The only problem is one steeply sloped area by some stairs. No matter what I do, it's still patchy and rain-gullied. The mud gets all over the stairs every time it rains. I've reseeded, fertilized, and reseeded again. I'm at a loss for what to try next.

WHAT YOU NEED:

Plants for Regions A & B

- **6 Miniature daffodils**
- **3 Baskets-of-gold**
- **50 Mixed sedum**
- **6 Miniature tulips**
- **4 Pinks (dianthus)**
- **3 Campanulas**
- **6 Ornamental grasses**
- **6 Snow-in-summer**
- **12 Impatiens**
- **15 Potentilla**
- **3 Euonymus**
- **10 Angel's tears**

Regional plant alternatives listed on pages 120-123. For suggested lawn care products, see page 113.

A: A rock garden might be good for stabilizing that steep slope. Place the largest rocks on the bottom, smaller rocks at the top, and slant them slightly inward for maximum stability. Follow the existing curve of the slope, and carry it out to where the slope ends naturally. Don't mortar the rocks—drainage is better without it. Backfill as you build organic matter and topsoil. Sprinkle the wall lightly to settle the soil, and add more soil behind and between the rocks. Sprinkle again, and press the soil in hard between the rocks. Continue until every crack and corner is crammed with soil.

Balance the effect with a rock-enclosed planting area on the opposite side of the stairs. Fill it with organic material and soil.

Fill in the space at the top and between the rocks with a collection of miniature bulbs and rock-garden classics. Tiny, charming bulbs include hoop-petticoat daffodil, yellow-flowered Hawera narcissus, angel's tears, English bluebell, violet-scented iris, and the miniature species tulips, *Tulipa dasystemon* and *T. batalini*. Showy rock-garden plants include pinks; dainty bellflowers, such as *Campanula portenschlagiana*, tussock bellflower, and *C. fragilis*; and basket-of-gold.

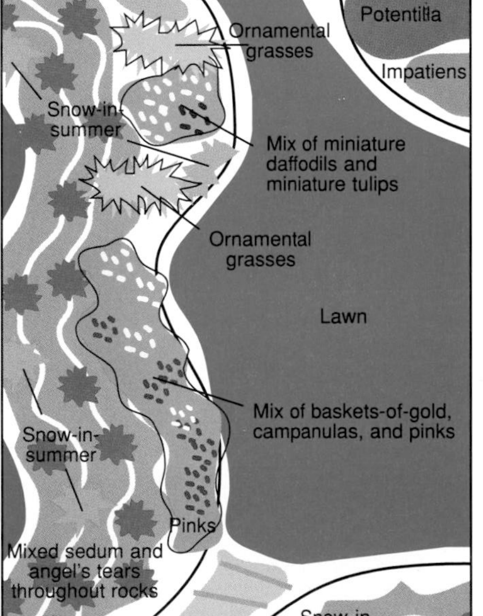

Landscape design by the Brickman Group, Langhorne, Pennsylvania

34 SPECIAL CONDITIONS
Along the Foundation

Q: My lawn grows right up to my house, but I'm having a difficult time keeping the part against the foundation neatly trimmed. The mower leaves a ragged edge, and I don't particularly enjoy crawling on my hands and knees with a pair of grass clippers. Is there another way to go about this?

A: Eliminate the problem entirely by carving out an attractively curved shrub and flower bed all along the front of the house. Emphasize the graceful curve with liriope (lilyturf). Behind it, mass mums for a dramatic fall show. In the spring, fill that space with red tulips and, in the summer, with tall, yellow African marigolds. A boxwood topiary in the form of a cone creates an exclamation point of emphasis for the corner of the flower display. Low-growing shrubs fill in the remainder of the foundation border.

WHAT YOU NEED:

Plants for Region B

- 1 Boxwood
- 20 Mums
- 32 Liriopes
- 6 Variegated mock orange
- 3 Mock orange

Regional plant alternatives listed on pages 120-123. For suggested lawn care products, see page 113.

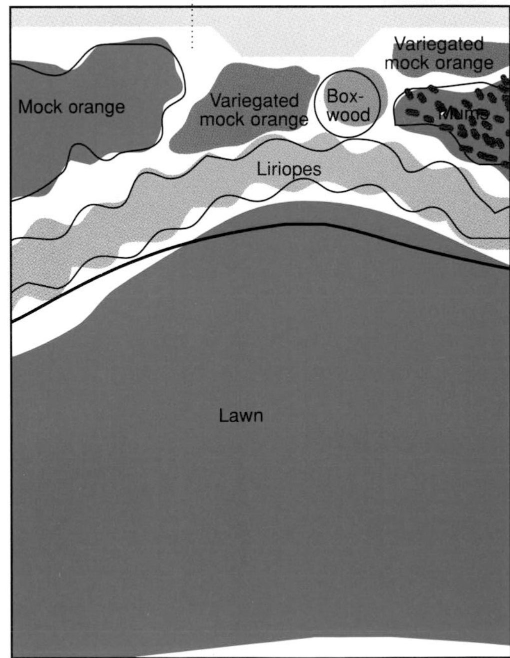

SPECIAL CONDITIONS
Along the Foundation

Q: We've just finished building our dream house in the South, complete with a formal entry. How do we carry that effect out in the landscaping, particularly along our shaded front-entry foundation?

A: Formal landscaping typically calls for straight lines and geometric shapes. Emphasize the formality of the entry with small, carefully clipped topiary trees at each side of the entry. Weeping fig, a good warm-climate choice, responds well to shaping. Echo that effect with two small flowering shrubs grown as standards (shrubs grown to have a single trunk and look like miniature trees). Azaleas, fuchsias, and roses all are available as standards. Since the climate is warm and the entry rather shaded, fuchsias are the best choice. They set off the entry dramatically when in bloom, and are attractive out of bloom as well.

A formal house demands a show-quality lawn and as broad an expanse of lawn as the lot allows. In Region C, plant drought-resistant St. Augustinegrass that produces a rich, dark green lawn.

Mowing and edging are essential to the formal, manicured look. Make the mowing easier by creating a foundation border filled with azaleas. Azaleas are spectacular when they flower and have a neat, formal look the rest of the year.

WHAT YOU NEED:

REGION

A B C

Plants for Region C

- **2 Weeping figs**
- **6 Nandinas**
- **8 Azaleas**
- **2 Fuchsias**
- **6 Impatiens**

Regional plant alternatives listed on pages 120-123. For suggested lawn care products, see page 113.

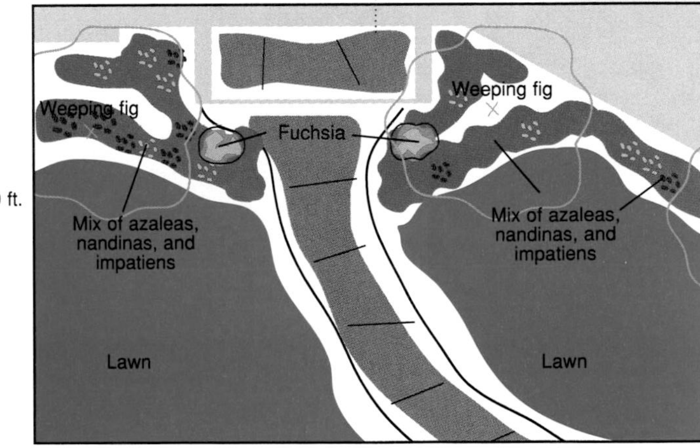

SPECIAL CONDITIONS
Along the Foundation

Q: We have just finished renovating our house—including repair to the foundation—and want to put it on the market. Unfortunately, the construction work left the front yard looking like a disaster area. What can we do to spruce up the yard quickly?

A: The quickest way to make a dramatic impact on the appearance of a house is to put in a fresh, new lawn. Lay out the shape of the new lawn to leave space for a foundation border and flower beds around the trees. These flower beds and foundation borders serve several purposes; they make for less mowing, they make for easier mowing, and they protect the trees from mower damage. In addition, flowers and flowering shrubs, such as hydrangeas, give the house more appeal.

In Region A, seed the new lawn with Scotts® Play for a thick, dark green lawn that establishes quickly and requires less watering and mowing than other turf grasses. In Region B, substitute Scotts Classic Estates®.

Fill the foundation border and the flower beds under the trees with fast-growing, long-blooming annuals. Marigolds, petunias, and geraniums are summer classics and will bloom before, with, and after the hydrangea, surrounding the house and lawn with flowers all summer long.

WHAT YOU NEED:

REGION

Plants for Regions A & B

10 Geraniums
1 Juniper
20 Petunias
8 Marigolds
1 Hydrangea

Regional plant alternatives listed on pages 120-123. For suggested lawn care products, see page 113.

40 ft.

54 ft.

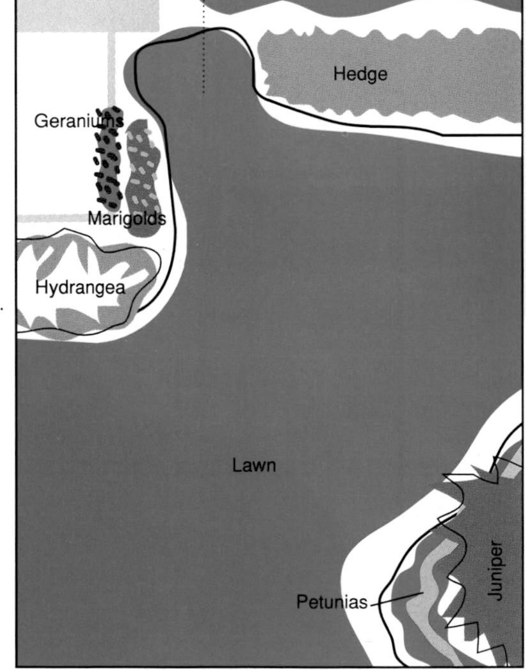

37 SPECIAL CONDITIONS
Around Corners

Q: We have a set of flagstone steps that curves from the driveway to a stepping-stone path that leads to the back yard. The lawn curves around the edges of the steps. The area is a nuisance to mow and always ends up looking ragged. What can we do?

A: Save yourself some trimming time and put in a small, curved border bed of shade-loving perennial variegated hostas interplanted in the summer with white impatiens. Before planting, amend the flower bed with Scotts® 3-in-1 Organic Mix.

This solution eliminates the need to mow the area, adds summer color, and makes an especially pretty accent to the flagstone steps.

For additional color on the steps, set out pots of wax begonias and caladium. Put pretty evergreens like yew, euonymus, and juniper near the house to create further interest.

WHAT YOU NEED:

REGION

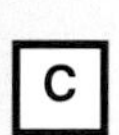

Plants for Regions A & B

- **6 Wax begonias**
- **7 Hostas**
- **30 Impatiens**
- **3 Caladiums**
- **1 Yew**
- **1 Euonymus**
- **2 Creeping junipers**

Regional plant alternatives listed on pages 120-123. For suggested fertilizers, see page 105.

12 ft.

21 ft.

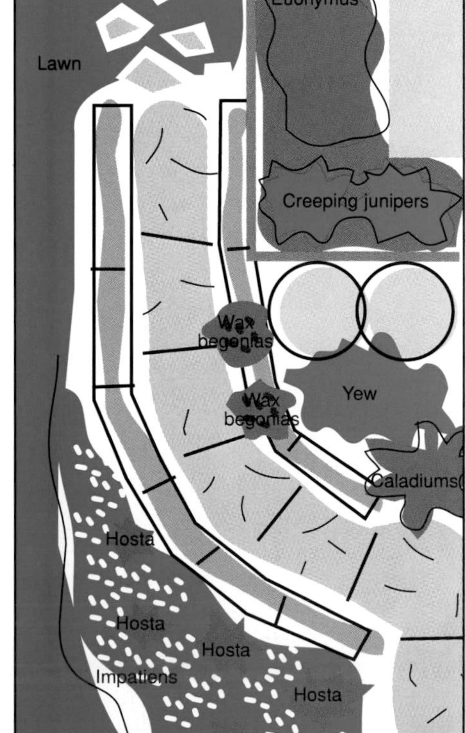

38 SPECIAL CONDITIONS
Edgings

Q: I guess everybody has one yard chore they just hate—mine is edging the lawn around the flower beds. Is there a self-edging lawn?

A: There aren't any self-edging lawns, but there is a simple way to get out of edging flower beds—grow flowers. Edging beds with flowers or foliage plants that grow just over the edge of the lawn hide the edge. Visually, it's no longer a problem because nobody can see it. Some good flower choices are hostas, dusty millers, and Madagascar periwinkles.

When you mow, carry a long, narrow piece of plywood with you. Use it to nudge the flowers out of way as you mow. If the lawn edges stay ragged, no one will ever know but you.

Since this is the garden equivalent of sweeping the dust under the carpet, you should do a proper edging at least once a year. The only time the edges are likely to show is in the spring before the flowers are established enough to cover them.

WHAT YOU NEED:

Plants for Region B

- 8 Lilies
- 2 Daylilies
- 4 Hostas
- 6 Wax begonias
- 1 Rose
- 1 Euryops
- 3 Dusty millers
- 1 Dogwood
- 2 Daisies

No alternative plants recommended. For suggested lawn care products, *see page 113.*

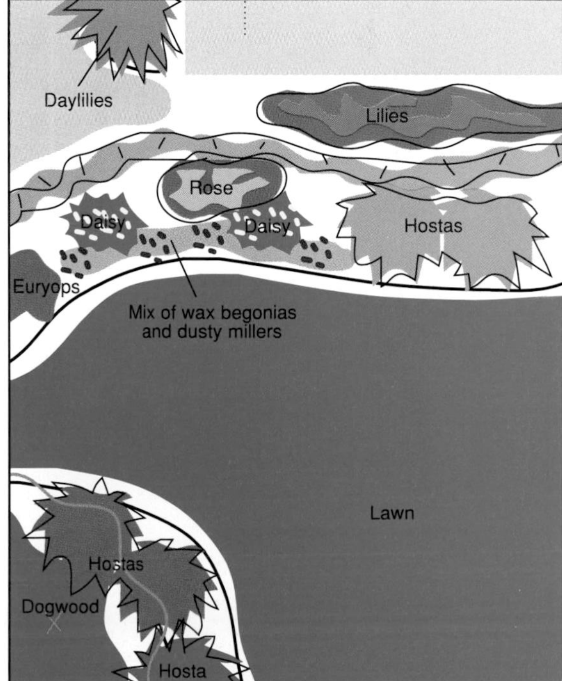

39 **SPECIAL CONDITIONS**
Edgings

Q: Our retirement dream was to buy a house in the Sun Belt. Now we've done it, but the previous owners' version of landscaping was brick and gravel, which we find both hot and ugly. What can we plant to cool things down without requiring a lot of work or high maintenance?

A: Leave the central brick area as an interestingly shaped patio, and build a circular brick planter in the center. Plant a small flowering tree, such as a flowering plum or crab apple, to provide some early spring bloom and a bit of light summer shade.

Have all the gravel raked up and removed. Around the edges of the yard and around any large trees, create attractively curved borders and fill them with a low-maintenance, flowering groundcover, such as dwarf periwinkle.

Edge the border with brick that matches the brick of the patio and house to pull everything together. If you like, plant another flowering fruit tree for bloom in the spring and dappled shade in the summer. Flowering pear would do well.

Fill in the remaining space with a lawn. Grass absorbs heat and cools the atmosphere dramatically. A good Sun Belt grass is Scotts® Sonesta Bermudagrass. It establishes quickly, does well in sunny situations, is an attractive dark green, and requires less watering and mowing than other kinds of grass. The bricks that edge the groundcover borders do double duty as a mowing edge, so it's no extra work to keep the edges of the lawn neat and tidy.

WHAT YOU NEED:

REGION

Plants for Regions B & C

1	**Crab apple tree**
5	**Ferns**
400	**Dwarf periwinkles**
1	**Pear tree**

Regional plant alternatives listed on pages 120-123. For suggested lawn care products, see page 113.

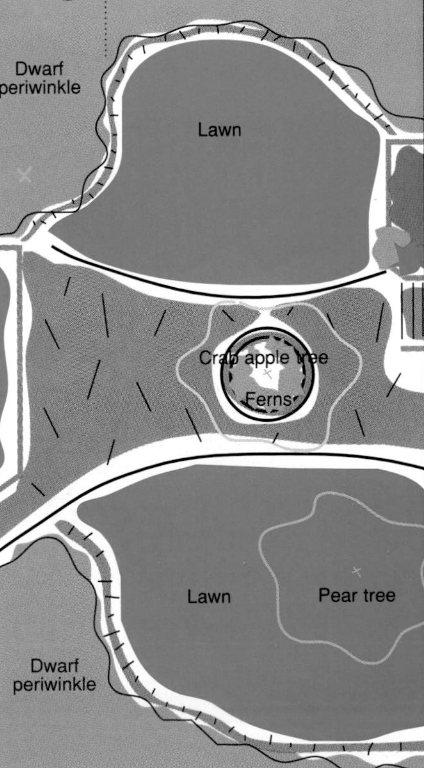

40 SPECIAL CONDITIONS Around Young Trees

Q: We have a clump of small birches alongside our house. I don't want just bare earth under the trees, but I'm afraid if I try to get a mower under there, I might nick and cut the young trees. What can I plant there that will be attractive?

A: Fill in the space around your trees with drifts of spring bulbs, perhaps yellow daffodils followed by yellow lily-flowered tulips. Plant a few carefully chosen rhododendrons and azaleas between the drifts. Overplant the bulbs with pink creeping phlox, and finish the whole thing off with an attractive mulch for a neat, orderly appearance. Use Scotts® Bulb Food when planting your bulbs for fuller, more beautiful plants and blooms.

The phlox puts on a dramatic show by itself, and, in concert with a matching pink azalea, the awkward space under your trees will become a showplace.

WHAT YOU NEED:

REGION

Plants for Regions A & B

- **1 White birch**
- **10 Tulips**
- **2 Barberries**
- **2 Rhododendrons**
- **2 Azaleas**
- **16 Creeping phlox**

Regional plant alternatives listed on pages 120-123. For suggested fertilizers, see page 105.

18 ft.

22 ft.

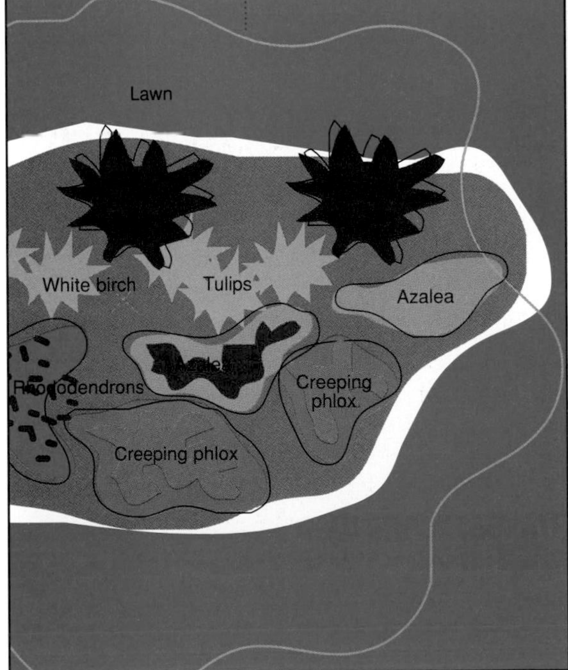

41 SPECIAL CONDITIONS
Around Mature Trees

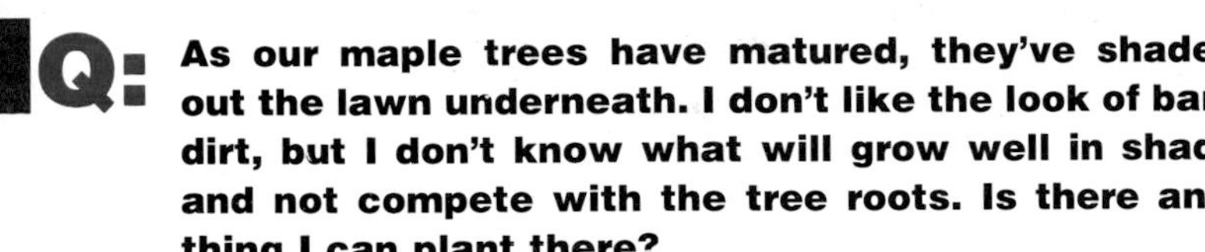

Q: As our maple trees have matured, they've shaded out the lawn underneath. I don't like the look of bare dirt, but I don't know what will grow well in shade and not compete with the tree roots. Is there anything I can plant there?

A: Spread a good, rich topsoil in a 2-inch layer under the tree. Where large tree roots don't interfere, plant bulbs of scilla (Spanish bluebell), and then overplant the bulbs with a shade-loving groundcover, such as periwinkle.

Cover the area with bark chips to give a tidy appearance until the periwinkle has filled in.

The Spanish bluebell sends up 20-inch stalks of blue flowers in the spring, and the periwinkle is covered with lavender-blue, pinwheel-shaped flowers in summer.

WHAT YOU NEED:

REGION

Plants for Region B

2 Paperbark maple trees
120 Periwinkles
20 Ferns
70 Scillas (Spanish bluebells)

Regional plant alternatives listed on pages 120-123. For suggested fertilizers, see page 105.

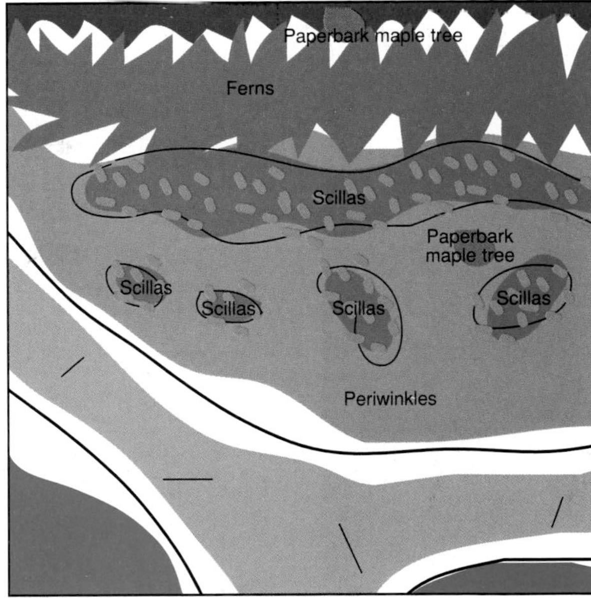

42 SPECIAL CONDITIONS
Around Mature Trees

Q: Dense shade from our deciduous trees has made the lawn under them sparse and thin. I love the trees, but I'm tired of raking leaves off the lawn every fall. Is there a way to have trees without the lawn looking patchy and the leaves piling up on my lawn?

A: One simple solution solves both problems; plant shade-loving, perennial groundcovers. In the shadiest areas, plant a hardy fern, such as common polypody. Space the clumps about 2 feet apart for good coverage.

Fill in the remainder of the space with Japanese spurge *(Pachysandra)*. Cover the area with an attractive mulch to keep the area looking neat until the groundcovers have covered the space completely.

Not only are these groundcovers easy to maintain, but because fallen leaves disappear under the groundcover, there's no longer much need to rake.

WHAT YOU NEED:

Plants for Regions B & C

175 Japanese spurge

100 Ferns

Regional plant alternatives listed on pages 120-123. For suggested fertilizers, see page 105.

15 ft.

20 ft.

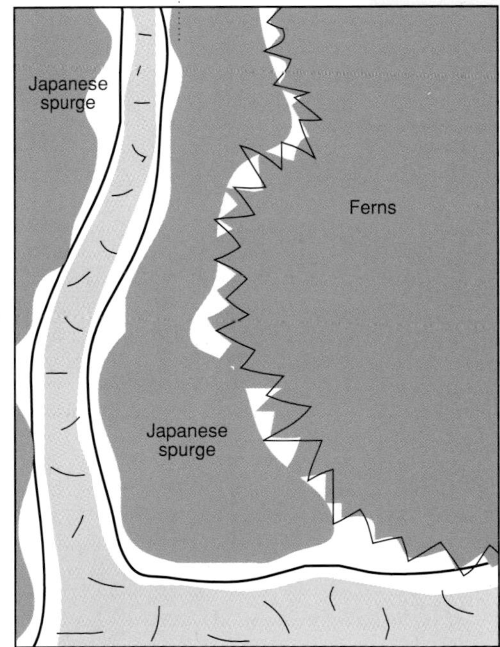

SPECIAL CONDITIONS
Poor Soil

Q: I have substantial areas of very poor, sandy soil off to one side of my back yard. I've planted parts of it with native ornamental grasses, but one large patch is in the middle of the lawn. The grass there always looks pale and weak. What can I do?

A: It probably would be more effective and more attractive to put in plants that thrive in poor, sandy soil. You'll find it easier to work with the land than against it.

Take out the portion of lawn that's not doing well. Dig in a generous helping of organic matter and peat moss to a depth of 8 to 10 inches. Scotts® 3-in-1 Organic Mix is a rich blend of organic material premixed for your convenience. Put in a collection of heaths, heathers, and evergreens. Heathers need fast drainage, which is exactly what sandy soil does best. They do best in acidic soil, which is why it's important to add some peat moss.

The hardiest heaths and heathers are those native to northern and western Europe, followed by those native to the Mediterranean region and southern Europe. The least-hardy heathers are native to South Africa; most will not tolerate temperatures much below freezing. Select heathers with a variety of different foliage colors, blooming seasons, and growth habits. By choosing carefully, it's possible to have color from flowers and foliage all year round.

WHAT YOU NEED:

REGION

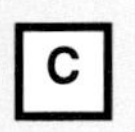

Plants for Regions A & B

- **1 Dwarf balsam fir**
- **2 Dwarf spruce**
- **1 Dwarf blue spruce**
- **5 Crimson pygmy barberries**
- **2 False cypresses**
- **1 Dwarf Alberta spruce**
- **30 Heaths and heathers**
- **1 Upright juniper**

Regional plant alternatives listed on pages 120-123. For suggested fertilizers, see page 105.

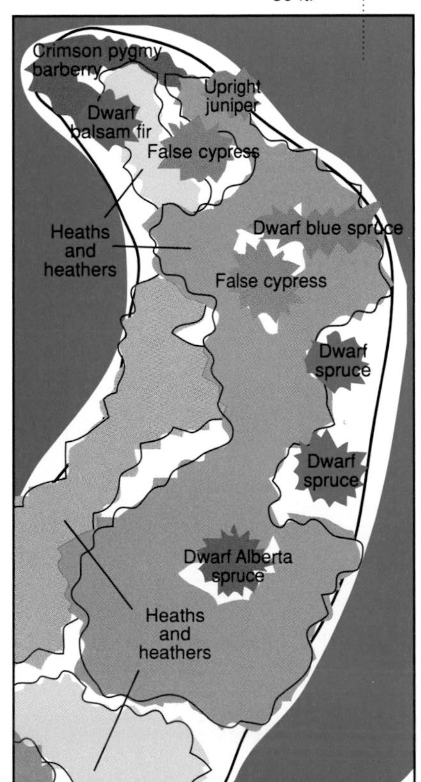

44 SPECIAL CONDITIONS
Poor Soil

Q: We recently bought a cottage by the sea. The existing landscape is *au natural*—a few native Coast live oaks and some struggling weeds. The soil is poor, but I'm determined to give this place a beautiful garden. Where should I begin?

A: Start by laying out wide flagstone paths, so you can walk comfortably to the best places to watch the surf crash and the sun set over the ocean. Pick the sunniest spot you have and lay out an interestingly shaped lawn. In Region B, plant zoysiagrass, which is excellent along the coast because it tolerates salt air well. For warmer areas in Region C, plant St. Augustinegrass. Since the soil is poor, make a practice of fertilizing the lawn regularly.

Trim out the lower twigs and branches of the Coast live oaks to open up the view and let in more light.

Underneath the oaks, put in flowers that aren't fussy about soil and that do well under coastal conditions—salt air, wind, fog, and humidity among them. For a flower border, combine Lily-of-the-Nile, California poppy, beach aster, Paris daisy, blue daisy, yellow daisy, statice, basket-of-gold, Regal geranium, and ivy geranium. Amend the flower bed heavily with organic matter and toss some fertilizer into each planting hole. For a shrub border, consider mock orange and all sorts of dwarf juniper. Amend the shrub border heavily with organic material. Try one of the Scotts® planting soils for a rich blend of organic materials.

WHAT YOU NEED:

Plants for Regions B & C

- **6 Junipers**
- **7 Mock oranges**
- **1 Japanese maple**

Regional plant alternatives listed on pages 120-123. For suggested lawn care products, see page 113.

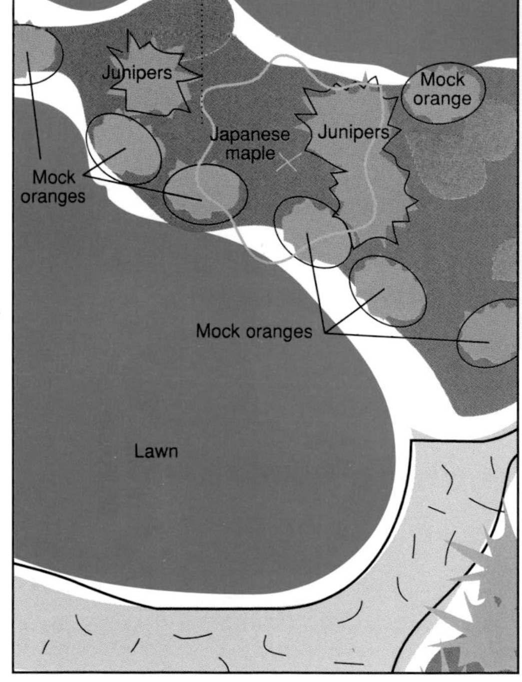

SPECIAL CONDITIONS
Poor Drainage

Q: Our house is located on a floodplain, and winter rains turn the front yard into a swamp. Except for one big maple, nothing much grows well. Short of planting cattails, what can we do?

WHAT YOU NEED:

REGION

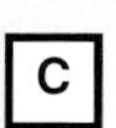

A B C

Plants for Region B

10 Azaleas
1 Mugo pine
1 Maple tree
1 Cedar
1 Dwarf Alberta spruce
2 Heavenly bamboo
2 Ferns

Regional plant alternatives listed on pages 120-123. For suggested lawn care products, see page 113.

A: Obviously, poor drainage is the biggest problem. Since water always runs downhill, regrade the front yard to slope away from the house so water will run off. (This is a major landscaping job. It's wise to hire a professional to do it.) At the base of the slope, create a small, winding, dry stream bed lined with river rock. It looks attractive through the dry months and, in the rainy season, carries excess water off in an orderly manner. (Again, consult with a landscape professional to make sure the water ends up flowing someplace socially acceptable—not onto the sidewalk.)

Once the site is regraded, amend the soil heavily for faster drainage. Dig in as much organic material as you can— shredded leaves or compost will help. Decide where along the sides you want to plant shrubs and flowers, and design your lawn around those spaces. Lay a lawn that will do well in both sun and the shade of that big maple. In Region B, a turf-type tall fescue provides a lush green lawn and grows well in moderate shade. Try Scotts® Classic Estates® for a thick green lawn.

Build up your perimeter beds and borders into berms (little hills) with a fast-draining soil mix. Both the slope and the soil will improve the drainage. Fill the berms in the shadow of the maple with shade-loving ferns, camellias, rhododendrons, and azaleas. Fill a berm in a sunny area with a collection of low-maintenance evergreens, such as dwarf cedars, spruces, and junipers.

Add shade-loving annuals in front of the azaleas for a burst of color spring through fall. The possibilities include Busy Lizzie impatiens, poor man's orchid, pansy, coleus, and tuberous begonia.

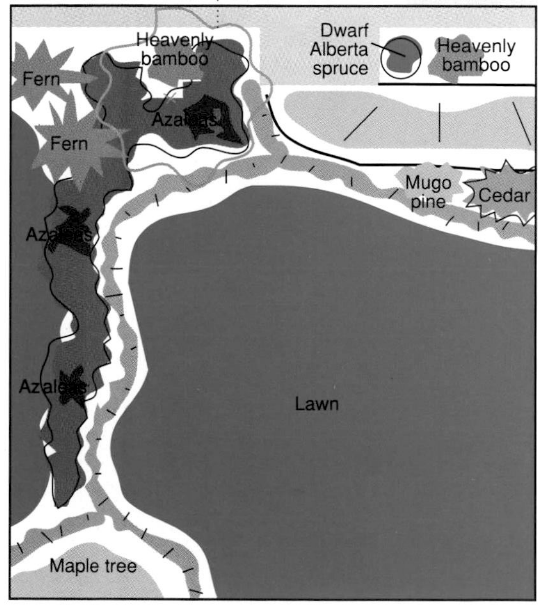

SPECIAL CONDITIONS
Around Water

Q: How do you landscape a bog? We have a delightful little pond on our property. Unfortunately, it is surrounded by a much less delightful, soggy perimeter. Mowing there is not practical. Any suggestions?

WHAT YOU NEED:

REGION

Plants for Regions A & B

- **3 Azaleas**
- **6 Irises**
- **6 Aquatic irises**
- **10 Forget-me-nots**
- **1 Dwarf Alberta spruce**
- **1 Fern**
- **6 Candytufts**

Regional plant alternatives listed on pages 120-123. For suggested lawn care products, see page 113.

A: Cut the lawn out of the boggy area and from around any trees. Besides keeping your feet dry, it will prevent trunk damage to the trees from the mower.

Prepare a planting bed by digging in lots of organic material, such as Scotts® 3-in-1 Organic Mix. Plant hardy, perennial bog plants, such as cardinal flower, yellow water iris, the exquisite Higo strain of Japanese iris, and hardy Louisiana iris. Yellow water iris spreads enthusiastically, so if you prefer something with a bit more restraint, substitute the *'Monstrosa'* iris, which has huge violet-and-white flowers. On the outer edges of the bog nearest the lawn, plant hardy, moisture-loving plants, such as goatsbeard, astilbe, azalea, and Himalayan cowslip. Outstanding moist-soil foliage plants include most Hosta hybrids, skunk cabbage, and the stupendous *Gunnera manicata*, with leaves 6 feet across. (Protect the *Gunnera* in winter by tying the leaves over the crown. Don't untie them until all danger of frost is past.)

For a groundcover, plant creeping Jenny (moneywort). It spreads fast and is covered with bright yellow, buttercup-like flowers all summer. If you think the creeping Jenny might be too invasive, mulch with bark chips instead for a tidy look.

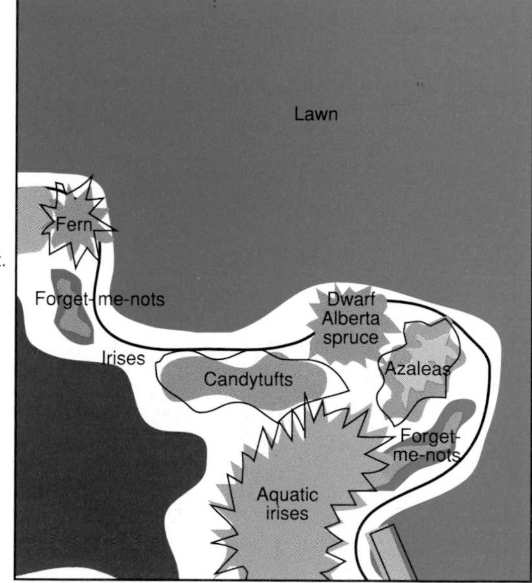

SPECIAL CONDITIONS
Winter Color

Q: My flower borders look pretty during our mild winters, but the grass turns an ugly brown color. Is there any way that I can have a green lawn in the winter without resorting to spraying it with green dye?

A: Lawns that are properly fertilized will hold their color significantly longer into the winter. For an annual feeding schedule that will keep your lawn greener, read about the Scotts® Turf Builder® Annual Program on page 111.

A second option for warm-season grasses, such as bermudagrass, is to overseed with a ryegrass. Plant ryegrass in the fall, and it will provide a lush green throughout the winter. The ryegrass will die out in spring when the bermudagrass begins to green up.

WHAT YOU NEED:

REGION

Plants for Region C

- **12 Zinnias**
- **18 Wax begonias**
- **18 Variegated geraniums**
- **24 Marigolds**
- **1 Portugal laurel**
- **1 Mock orange**

Regional plant alternatives listed on pages 120-123. For suggested lawn care products, see page 113.

35 ft.

50 ft.

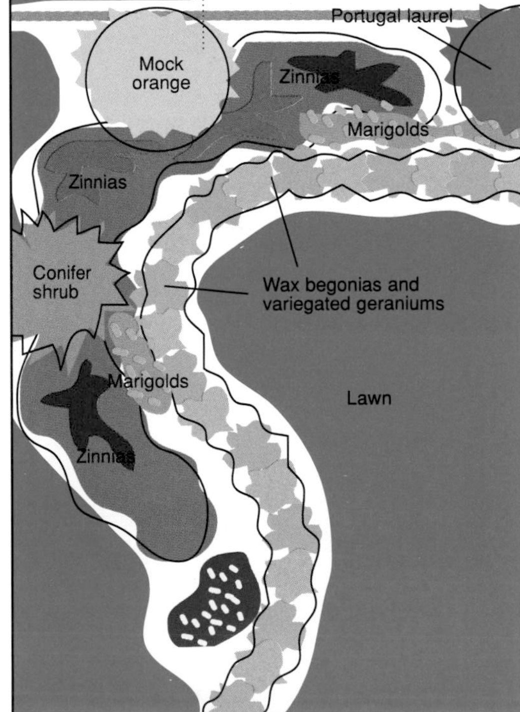

SPECIAL CONDITIONS
Winter Color

Q: **I maintain the grounds and turf on a large estate. Because the lawns are such an important part of the showplace effect, it is essential they look healthy and green all year. I am already growing St. Augustinegrass. Is there anything else I can do to prevent winter browning?**

A: St. Augustinegrass will stay green in many mild climates throughout the year. You can keep your lawn greener in the winter by properly fertilizing it. Many homeowners think of fertilizing as a spring activity. However, applying a fertilizer in the fall, such as Scotts® Winterizer or Turf Builder®, will keep your lawn greener longer in winter and give you a faster green-up in the spring.

WHAT YOU NEED:

REGION

Plants for Regions B & C

10 Junipers
12 Mondo grasses
6 Water lilies

Regional plant alternatives listed on pages 120-123. For suggested lawn care products, see page 113.

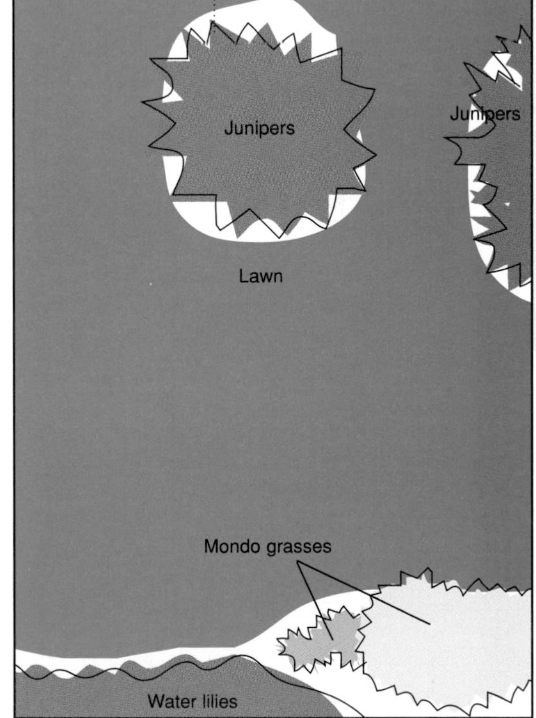

49

SPECIAL CONDITIONS
High Traffic

Q: We are putting in an elaborate play set for our children, complete with swings, crossing bars, a slide, and more. I don't know if grass can stand up to the kind of punishment the kids are likely to inflict. Is there anything I can do to ensure that it will?

A: Grass makes an excellent play surface for children, since the inevitable tumbles don't result in painful scrapes. Choose a grass that is specially formulated for heavy traffic, such as Scotts® Classic Estates®, a fast-germinating mix for hard-use areas in Region B. It creates a durable lawn that resists weeds, which means it takes less work to keep it looking attractive. In Region C, choose St. Augustinegrass.

In addition to being the most kid-friendly surface possible under play equipment, grassy areas are excellent for children's games—from catch to tag. They're also easy to incorporate back into the rest of the landscape when the children outgrow the play set.

WHAT YOU NEED:

REGION

A B

C

Plants for Regions B & C

- **1 Palm tree**
- **12 Petunias**
- **50 Impatiens**

Regional plant alternatives listed on pages 120-123. For suggested lawn care products, see page 113.

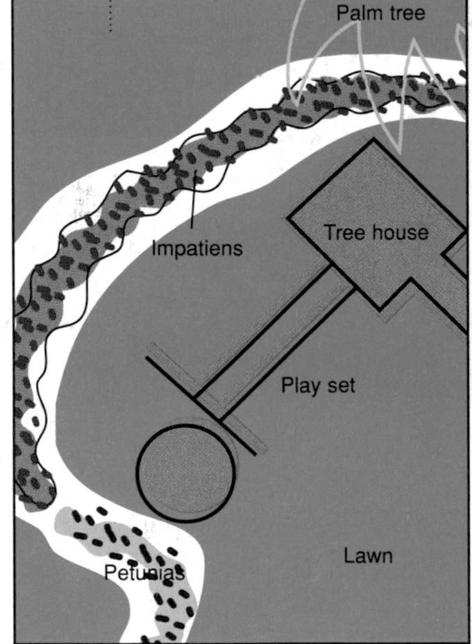

50 **SPECIAL CONDITIONS**
High Traffic

Q: **Everyone who comes or goes from our house walks across the lawn. The portion that leads to the front door looks like an elephant trail. Should I replace the lawn with a grass mixture specially formulated for hard-use, high-traffic areas? How will that look with the rest of the lawn?**

A: Sometimes the easy way out is also the wisest decision. For that kind of traffic stream, add a path of stepping-stones level with the lawn from the driveway to the front door. Reseed the area with Scotts® PatchMaster® Bermudagrass/Ryegrass Lawn Repair Mix. Once it's nicely grown in, you can mow it as you do the rest of the lawn; the lawn mower will go right over the stepping-stones without a problem.

WHAT YOU NEED:

REGION

B

Plants for Region C

- **5 Mock oranges**
- **1 Yew pine**
- **1 Heavenly bamboo**
- **1 Bougainvillea**
- **3 Fortnight lilies**

Regional plant alternatives listed on pages 120-123. For suggested lawn care products, see page 113.

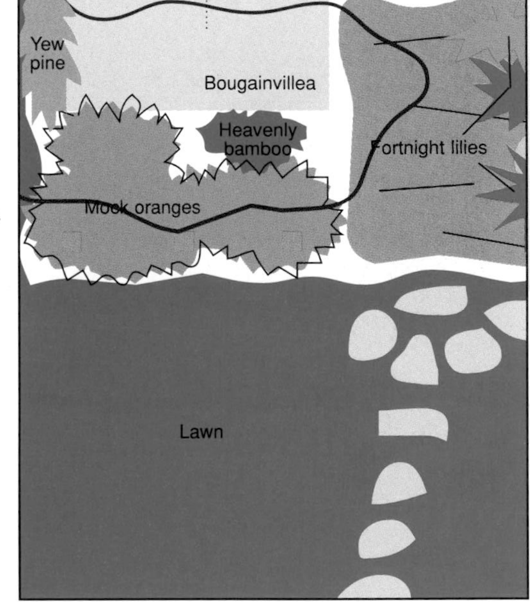

Lawn and Groundcover Basics

WHETHER YOU'RE NEW TO LAWN AND GROUNDCOVER GARDENING OR YOUR GREEN THUMB is fading, rely on this chapter for helpful advice. We begin with a discussion of soil composition and fertility. Following that is planting and maintenance information for all of the different grass types and groundcovers.

ANALYZING THE CONDITIONS IN YOUR YARD

Good soil is as important to your lawn and garden as a good foundation is to your house. And just as your house has a plan you like, your landscape can have one, too. But before you take spade to soil, there are a few things you need to know about your soil—especially its composition and fertility.

Soil is composed of four primary ingredients: sand, clay, silt, and organic matter, or humus. Your soil type is determined by its proportions of these four materials. If you have too much clay in your soil, it will not till or drain well. If you have too much sand in your soil, it won't retain enough moisture for your plants to grow. If you pick up a handful of your soil and you can squeeze it into a tight, sticky mass, it is high in clay. A loose, crumbly soil that won't hold any shape has a high sand content. The ideal soil is a dark, light mixture of sand, clay, and a generous helping of organic material.

The best way to improve your soil's physical characteristics is to work in organic matter (or humus), such as Scotts® 3-in-1 Organic Mix. If you add organic matter to sandy soil, it will improve water retention. If you add it to clay soil, it improves drainage and workability. However, because none of these organic materials contains many plant nutrients, you shouldn't use them in place of fertilizer.

Loam (top), the ideal soil, molds into a loose mound when squeezed lightly. Squeezed harder, however, it crumbles. Sandy soil (center) feels grainy and crumbles when wet. Soil high in clay (bottom) forms a tight, sticky mass if squeezed when wet.

FERTILIZING YOUR GARDENS

Soil fertility is just as important to your garden as soil composition. Consider these products when improving your soil:

Scotts Granular Plant Foods: Scotts granular plant foods are slow-release fertilizers that can be mixed in with the soil when planting or simply spread around established plants.

Scotts Ready-to-Use Liquids: Scotts ready-to-use liquid is a snap to use. Simply connect it to your hose and spray. Promote vigorous plants and beautiful blooms with these handy fertilizers.

Peters® Professional® Plant Foods: Peters water-soluble plant foods are the same products three out of four professional growers prefer to use. Peters plant foods are fully soluble so no clogging occurs in your feeder. Peters rich feeding of nitrogen, phosphorus, potassium, and micronutrients produces full, lush plants that will be the envy of your neighbors.

Once® Season-Long Plant Foods: Once Season-Long plant foods are granular fertilizers that produce a slow-release feeding of primary nutrients and minor nutrients for an entire plant season. Just apply this fertilizer once and get beautiful blooms and lush foliage for the entire season.

Osmocote® Plant Foods: Osmocote plant foods provide the ultimate in extended-release fertilizers. These products provide your plants a balanced diet for up to a full year. This convenient line of fertilizers allows you to feed your plants once a season without the danger of over- or underfeeding.

Note: Groundcovers fall into many different plant categories. Feed groundcovers according to the plant group to which they belong—for example, perennials or woody plants.

FERTILIZER CHART

Plant Group	Feeding Schedule*	Scotts Granular Plant Foods	Scotts Ready-to-Use Liquids	Peters Professional Water Solubles	Once Season-Long Plant Foods	Osmocote Plant Foods
Annuals	*Spring and Summer*	Flower Food	Rose & Flowering Shrub Plant Food	All-Purpose Plant Food or Super Blossom Booster	Vegetables & Bedding Plants	Vegetable & Bedding Plant Food
Berries	*Prior to Spring Growth*	Fruit and Berry Food	All-Purpose Plant Food	All-Purpose Plant Food	Vegetables & Bedding Plants	Outdoor & Indoor Plant Food
Bulbs, Tubers	*Planting Time and After Flowering*	Bulb Food	All-Purpose Plant Food	All-Purpose Plant Food	Roses & Flowering Plants	Vegetable & Bedding Plant Food
Evergreens	*Late Spring and Fall*	Evergreen Shrub & Tree Food	Azalea, Evergreen, Rhododendron, Holly Plant Food	All-Purpose Plant Food	Trees, Shrubs, & Evergreens	Tree & Shrub Planting Tablets
Perennials	*Early Spring and Mid-Summer*	Flower Food	Rose & Flowering Shrub Plant Food	All-Purpose Plant Food or Super Blossom Booster	Roses & Flowering Plants	Outdoor & Indoor Plant Food
Trees	*Late Spring and Fall*	Evergreen Shrub & Tree Food	All-Purpose Plant Food	All-Purpose Plant Food	Trees, Shrubs, & Evergreens	Tree & Shrub Planting Tablets
Palms	*Spring, Summer, and Fall*	Palm Food				
Woody Plants (such as Shrubs & Trees)	*Early Spring*	All-Purpose Plant Food	Azalea, Evergreen, Rhododendron, Holly Plant Food	All-Purpose Plant Food	Trees, Shrubs, & Evergreens	Tree & Shrub Planting Tablets
Azaleas, Camellias, Rhododendrons	*Early Spring and Summer*	Azalea, Camellia, Rhododendron Food	Azalea, Evergreen, Rhododendron, Holly Plant Food	Azalea, Camellia, Rhododendron Food	Roses & Flowering Plants	Outdoor & Indoor Plant Food
Roses	*Early Spring, Late Spring, and Mid-Summer*	Rose Food	Rose & Flowering Shrub Plant Food	Rose Food	Roses & Flowering Plants	Outdoor & Indoor Plant Food

** Always read fertilizer instructions prior to feeding.*

STARTING A LAWN

PREPARING THE SOIL

As with gardens, soils for lawns must have the proper composition and fertility. But first, the soil must be brought to the appropriate level in relation to the house and driveway, and must slope away from the house for proper drainage. If you are putting in a lawn from scratch, it's wise to hire a landscape professional to do the rough grading, install a sprinkler system, improve drainage, if necessary, and do the final grading. Check with local authorities about the location of any underground utility lines.

GRADING THE YARD

Establish a rough grade by filling in any low places and leveling any high spots. Distribute the soil so that elevation changes between such fixed points as the house, driveway, sidewalks, or existing trees are gradual rather than abrupt. Be certain the lawn slopes away from the house foundation.

To protect existing trees, avoid adding or removing more than 2 inches of soil within the drip line of large trees. It may be wiser to mulch or plant shade-loving shrubs and flowers at the base of trees than to try to establish grass there.

Before you begin seeding your lawn, be sure to smooth out high and low spots in the soil. Also, remove stones and other debris.

Measure the lawn area and make a note of the dimensions. This information is helpful in determining the amount of topsoil, soil amendments, grass seed, or sod you need.

If additional soil is required, spread topsoil or organic materials over the rough grade and till it in with a rotary tiller. Rotary tillers can be rented from equipment-rental stores. This also is the time to work in lime or gypsum if the results of your soil test indicate they're required. As a final step before seeding, spread Scotts® Starter® Fertilizer on the soil surface.

SEEDING

In most locations, the best time to seed a lawn is early in the fall, after the heat of summer and before heavy frost. The next best time is in the spring after the last killing frost and before hot weather sets in. Seed is sold as straight varieties, mixtures, and blends. Straight varieties are all one type of grass.

SCOTTS GRASS SEED CHART

Region A	Region B	Region C
Sports Turf		
Tri-Blend Tall Fescue	Tri-Blend Tall Fescue	
Picture		
Shady		
Family		
Play		
Classic Estates	Classic Estates	
Mirage Dwarf Tall Fescue	Mirage Dwarf Tall Fescue	
Sun Mix		
Shade Mix		
Sun & Shade Mix		
Quick Fix	Quick Fix	Quick Fix
Golf Course Blend	Golf Course Blend	Golf Course Blend
California Classic	California Classic	
Lawn Repair Kit	Lawn Repair Kit	
Kentucky Bluegrass		
Chesapeake Tall Fescue	Chesapeake Tall Fescue	
Contractors Mix	Contractors Mix	Contractors Mix
Landscapers Mix		
Perennial Ryegrass	Perennial Ryegrass	Perennial Ryegrass
Fall Grass Seed		
Aztec Tall Fescue		
PatchMaster Sun/Shade		
PatchMaster Tall Fescue	PatchMaster Tall Fescue	
	Sonesta Bermudagrass	Sonesta Bermudagrass
	Bermuda	Bermuda
	PatchMaster Bermuda/Rye	PatchMaster Bermuda/Rye

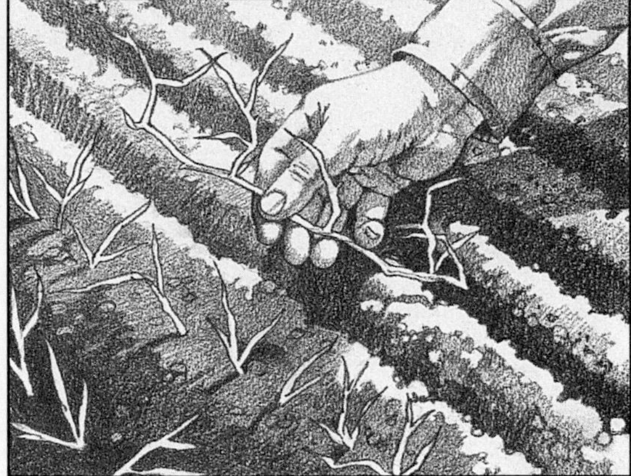

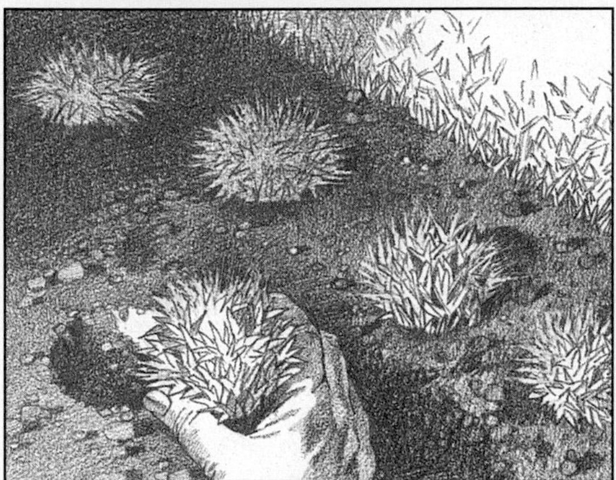

Top: Sprigging is one way to establish a new lawn. Bury individual sprigs so the uppermost nodes show above the ground.

Center: When using lawn plugs, it's wise to sprinkle some Starter Fertilizer into each planting hole.

Bottom: Lay sod as you would lay bricks—so that the seams are not lined up with each another. Once the sod is in place, you'll need to water it daily—more often if it is very hot—for six weeks, until the grass roots are firmly established.

Warm-season lawns, like bermudagrass hybrids, are often sold this way (Scotts Sonesta Bermudagrass Seed, for example). Mixtures contain seed from two or more types of grasses. A widely used cool-season mixture includes Kentucky bluegrass, fine fescue, and perennial ryegrass. Blends are a combination of cultivars from a single kind of grass. Most seed is sold as a mixture, so you can enjoy the strong individual characteristics of all the grass types that work well together.

Water a day or two before seeding and let the top inch of soil dry out. To sow the seed as evenly as possible, use a lawn spreader, then apply Scotts Starter Fertilizer. Rake lightly with a steel-tined rake to scratch the seeds into the soil. It's not necessary to cover every seed.

Water gently and thoroughly with a fine-mist spray, taking care not to wash out the seed. Keep the lawn moist by watering five to 10 minutes two to three times a day. If the weather is hot or windy, it may be necessary to water three or four times a day to maintain the evenly moist soil the seeds need to sprout. Don't mow until the lawn is one-third taller than you plan to keep the grass.

SODDING

Sod comes in rolls like carpet; each strip measures from 5 to 9 feet long and weighs about 30 pounds. Unlike seeded lawns, sod can be installed virtually any time of year and will be established within two weeks. But avoid the hot summer months or you'll need to water a lot. To order sod, determine the area of your lawn and add 10 percent.

Prepare the area exactly as you would if you were seeding a lawn. To check the quality of the sod, unroll a few pieces. It should be evenly moist and of an even thickness (1 inch thick is ideal). Pieces should be cleanly sliced, not ragged at the edges. Look for a good mat of roots on the underside. The blades should be dense and all of the same length.

Apply Scotts Starter Fertilizer on the soil surface and rake lightly. Lay the sod like bricks, so that seams are not lined up with each other. Press edges together tightly. Roll sod with a roller half filled with water to press roots into contact with the soil. Water daily for six weeks—more often if the weather is hot.

WARM-SEASON GRASS VARIETIES

Variety	Characteristics	Light	Mowing Height	Comments
BAHIAGRASS *Paspalum notatum*	Very coarse pasture grass; open habit; inexpensive to start but poorer quality. Erect and tough. Wide leaves. Seed heads unsightly in spring. Resists pests and diseases. Open to weeds.	Sun	2-3"	Tolerates partial shade, neglect, drought, moist and humid conditions, and acidic or alkaline soil. Turns brown below 30°F. Start by seed or sod. Slow to germinate (20 days) and establish. Popular in Southeast. Improved varieties include 'Paraguay,' 'Pensacola.,' 'Seaside,' 'Tifhi,' and Wilmington.'
BERMUDA-GRASS *Cynodon dactylon* 'Sonesta' 'Sahara'	Tough, attractive lawn, if given care. 'Tif' series grasses are dwarf and fine-textured, medium to dark green. Browns at 32°F. Overseeding with fine fescues or ryegrasses gives year-round green and keeps out weeds when dormant.	Sun	½-1½"	Does not like shade or cold, but resists drought and salt air and wears fairly well. Needs frequent mowing and feeding, and can invade flower beds. Subject to nematodes in Southeast, eriophyid mite in Southwest. Named varieties must be started from sprigs, stolons, or plugs. Wears well; used for athletic fields. Easy walking. Best water-use efficiency of all turf grasses.
'Santa Ana' 'Tifgreen' 'Tifway'	Medium texture, blue-green. Used on putting greens. One of the best 'Tifs'; used on fairways. Dark green; tolerates colder temperatures.	Sun Sun Sun	½-1½" ½-1½" ½-1½"	Resists salt and smog. Tolerates pollution. Frequent feedings brighten color. Stiffer; good for home lawns. Needs less mowing and care.
BUFFALO-GRASS	Very drought-tolerant; light greyish-green color; fine leaves.	Sun or light shade	¾-2"	Cold- and heat-tolerant. Becomes dormant below 32°F or during drought periods. Can survive longer drought periods than any other turf species, but isn't especially good in water-use efficiency.
CENTIPEDE-GRASS *Eremochloa ophiuroides* Chinese lawn grass	Medium green; medium texture, not as fine as bermudagrass. Tolerates less cold than bermudagrass but more than St. Augustinegrass. Spreads by creeping stems. Mow infrequently.	Sun	1½"	Not as tolerant of drought; discolors more readily. Well-adapted to infertile, acidic soils of Southeast from Carolinas south. Needs little feeding; give phosphorus and potassium only when dormant. Start by sprigs or plugs 1 to 1½ feet apart. Water regularly. Not good on seashore.
ST. AUGUSTINE-GRASS *Stenotaphrum secundatum*	Broad, flat stems; attractive blue-green nearly year-round. Thick, coarse stems; the best of the warm-season grasses for partial shade. Few seed heads.	Sun or shade	½-2"	Almost as fast-growing from plugs as bermudagrass. Tends to build up spongy thatch that makes walking on it difficult. Invasive. Subject to brown patch, grey-leaf spot, nematodes, St. Augustine Decline (SAD) virus, and chinch bugs. Needs spraying for proper care.
'Bitter Blue' 'Floratam' 'Seville' 'DelMar'	Blue-green; frost-tolerant. Dark green; resists virus & chinch bugs. Shade- and cold-tolerant. Shade- and cold-tolerant.	Same Same Same Same	½-2" ½-2" ½-2" ½-2"	Does not wear well. Poor tolerance to cold or shade. Resists SAD and grey-leaf spot, not chinch bugs. Resists SAD and grey-leaf spot, not chinch bugs.
ZOYSIA *Zoysia* sp. Wide-leaf 'Emerald' 'Meyer' 'Belair' 'El Toro'	Dark green; hardiest of the warm-season grasses; slow-growing but eventually dense. Grows as far north as Ohio but turns brown there from fall frost to last spring frost (six months). Can be overseeded with a grass, such as ryegrass, for winter green. Good green all summer.	Sun	¾-2"	Very dense growth does not lend to overseeding, though some success is developing with tall fescue mixes. Start zoysia from named-variety sprigs or plugs set 6-12" apart in spring. May take two seasons to fill in completely. Water during drought. Remove thatch and spray as needed for pests and diseases.
Fine-leaf 'Cashmere'	Looks like fine bermudagrass but is less invasive.	Sun	¾-2"	More shade-tolerant and considerably faster-growing than other zoysias.

SPRIGGING

Sprigs, also called stolons or runners, are pieces of grass stems and roots used to start lawns. Each sprig has roots or two to four joints from which roots can grow. Sprigging is a good way to start warm-season grasses. Sprigs are most often sold by the bushel by sod farms. The number needed per square-foot depends on the type of grass being planted.

It's essential to keep the sprigs cool and moist until they're planted. When planting, keep surplus sprigs in a cool, shaded place until they're needed.

Plant sprigs in the early spring, after all danger of frost is past. Prepare the seedbed as for seeding a lawn and scatter the sprigs by hand evenly over the soil. Cover the sprigs lightly with soil and roll the area with a cleated roller or a half-filled water roller. (Nurseries that sell sprigs usually have rollers for rent.) Fertilize the area with Scotts® Starter Fertilizer. Water gently and thoroughly. Keep the soil surface moist until the sprigs show active growth.

COOL-SEASON GRASS VARIETIES

Variety	Characteristics	Light	Mowing Height	Comments
BENTGRASS *Agrostis* sp. **Creeping**	Fine-quality, fine-textured turf. Aggressive; tolerates very low mowing height. Preferred turf for golf courses.	Sun	1/4-3/4"	Very susceptible to disease; has high water and nutrient requirements. Not suited to home lawns.
Colonial	Fine-textured. Not as aggressive as creeping bentgrass. Tolerates low fertility and acid soils. Prefers cooler, moist conditions.	Sun	1-2"	Used in mixtures with fine fescue in Northwest and Northeast.
BLUEGRASS *Poa pratensis*	Excellent turf-forming species. Spreads by underground rhizomes.	Sun	1½-2"	Highly recommended, at least as a component in a mix, for Region A. Varieties such as 'Abbey,' 'Ascot,' 'Bristol,' 'Coventry,' and 'Victa' are highly disease-resistant. 'Ascot,' 'Bristol,' and 'Coventry' are also shade-tolerant. Seed is relatively slow to germinate and establish.
FESCUE *Festuca* sp. Tall (coarse)	Medium green, coarse-bladed, clump-forming. Resists disease and drought. Tolerates a shortage of nutrients. Best for play areas that get rough treatment. Some varieties contain endophytic fungus, so they require less insecticide.	Sun or shade	2-3"	Highly recommended in Region B, where summers are hot and dry. Varieties such as 'Adobe,' 'Aztec,' and 'Mirage' are darker green, lower-growing, and finer-textured than others. 'Adobe' contains endophytic fungus, which means less insecticide.
Fine (chewings, red, creeping red, and hard fescues)	This group of four species is five-bladed and medium green in color. All tolerate shade, drought, low-nutrient soils, and sandy and acidic soil conditions. Some varieties contain endophytic fungus and require less insecticide. Large seeds; germinates in a few days. Coarse. Dies out in winter in the North, in summer in the South.	Sun or shade	2-3"	Often used for about 20-60% of mix with bluegrass or ryegrass to enhance shade and drought tolerance. Germinates faster than bluegrass, but compatible. More susceptible to heat and disease than coarse fescue. Useful for temporary lawn or as green manure to turn under and improve soil. Also good for overseeding dormant, warm-season grasses in fall.
RYEGRASS *Lolium* sp. Annual, Italian	Medium to dark green. Dense, fine-textured turf; almost equal to bluegrass but doesn't mow as neatly.	Sun	1½"	Often sown in mixtures with bluegrass. Rye sprouts more quickly and becomes established quicker. Makes a usable lawn in three weeks.
Perennial	Some varieties contain endophytic fungus and so require less insecticide.	Sun or light shade	1½"	Useful for overseeding dormant bermudagrass. Use new cultivars: 'Accolade,' 'Achiever,' and 'Divine.' All contain endophytic fungus, so they require less insecticide.

PLUGGING

Plugging is the process of digging holes in the seedbed and planting small round or square pieces of sod. Like sprigging, it is used only for warm-season grasses. Sod plugs 2 to 3 inches across with an active root system are sold 18 to a tray. One tray will plant 50 square feet. The plugs are sold by nurseries and garden centers. Plugs should be planted in early spring. The roots spread and quickly fill the lawn, providing a lush, green cover.

Prepare the seedbed as for seeding a lawn. Be sure the soil is moist before planting, and prevent the plugs from drying out by watering them often until they are planted. Steel sod pluggers or plug augers are available from most rental-equipment firms. These tools make straight-sided holes exactly the size of the plug, so the plug can be slipped easily into the soil. Add a small amount of Scotts Starter Fertilizer to each hole before planting.

Space the holes 12 to 18 inches apart, and offset the rows like a chessboard. Press the plugs firmly into the holes to make sure there are no air pockets between the roots and the soil. Plugs should be flush with the ground. Spread additional Starter Fertilizer on the soil surface.

Water gently and thoroughly immediately after planting. Water daily for the first two weeks to keep the plugs from drying out. After that, water every other day for a month.

Begin mowing once the plugs are well-rooted. Mowing encourages the plugs to spread. Fertilize every six to eight weeks with Scotts Turf Builder® until the lawn is completely filled in.

MAINTAINING A LAWN

Beautiful lawns don't just happen. They are made. And making them can be as simple as doing a few right things at the right times. That's the key to lawn success: Meeting the lawn's needs on a regular basis. It's called lawn programming.

THREE BASIC NEEDS

Although every lawn is different, all lawns have three basic needs that must be met on a regular basis. These needs are fertilizing, mowing, and watering.

From time to time, most lawns also need control of weeds and insects, which also can become a part of the lawn program.

Taking care of the fertilizing (as well as weed and insect control, if needed) may require as little as a half-hour, three or four times a year, for a typical 5,000-square-foot lawn.

Mowing and watering, on the other hand, must be done throughout the growing season, from spring through late fall. How often depends a great deal upon how much rainfall occurs.

It is the cumulative effect of the three lawn basics that lays the groundwork for a nice lawn. The following summaries are designed to help you get maximum benefit from each of these important steps.

A hand spreader broadcasts grass seed or granular fertilizers and weed-killers evenly, avoiding clumps of grass seed or missed spots in the lawn.

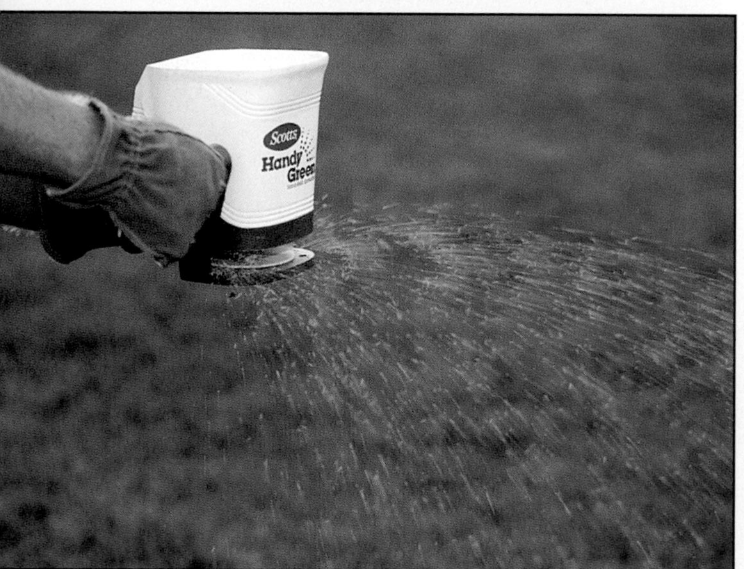

FERTILIZING

A program of fertilizing ensures a constant nutrient supply to your lawn. Occasional, hit-or-miss feedings may green up a lawn temporarily, but to get lasting green and a true thickening of the turf, nutrients must be available for the grass plants throughout the year. That is why every lawn needs feeding—not just once, but several times throughout the growing season. For example:

Early spring. Every good feeding program begins in early spring, to stimulate early green-up and to encourage the underground root development that produces a thick, green lawn above ground.

Late spring. If a controlled-release fertilizer, such as Scotts® Turf Builder®, is used, each feeding will last up to two months. So the second feeding will not be needed until late spring. This will continue the thickening process and carry the spring green into summer.

Summer. About two months later, in midsummer, a third feeding will provide nourishment during one of the most difficult times for grass plants—when temperatures are at their peak.

Fall. The fall feeding is one of the most important of the year—not only to repair summer damage and revitalize the grass plants, but also to prepare the lawn for the cold winter that lies ahead. (See feeding program on the opposite page and product recommendations on page 113.)

MOWING

Many homeowners take mowing for granted, not realizing how much effect it has on the appearance of the lawn. There are only a few mowing guidelines, but each plays an important part in the lawn's appearance:

Start early. Early in the spring, before the grass starts to grow, lower the mower blade and mow to remove as much dead grass as possible. This lets sunlight reach the crowns of the grass plants to trigger early greening.

Mow often. When grass is growing, mow at least once a week—more often when there has been heavy rainfall that makes the grass grow faster. The important thing is not to let the grass get so high that you must remove more than about one-third of the grass-blade length by mowing. Cutting off more causes plant stress and creates heavy clippings.

Keep blades sharp. Dull mower blades tear and shred grass blades. After a few days, the damaged grass turns brown. The remedy? Keep mower blades sharp throughout the season.

Not too low! After the first spring mowing, raise the height of the mower blade to about 2 inches for most lawn grasses (except hybrid bermuda or dichondra). Then, in hot weather, raise the height at least another ½ to 1 inch. Mowing too low can stress the lawn. When in doubt, mow at a high setting.

What about clippings? As municipalities move to restrict or ban the disposal of grass clippings in landfills, a common question is whether or not to remove the clippings from your lawn after mowing. Clippings can be removed from the lawn if they are either composted or removed by a waste-removal service. However, they also can be left to decompose on the lawn if mowing is done regularly so that clippings don't pile up and smother the grass.

The key to uniform lawn growth is to use granular, slow-release fertilizers, such as Scotts Turf Builder products. Applying this type of fertilizer to your lawn allows the grass plants to grow evenly throughout the season, without surge growth and without creating extra clippings.

Turf Builder® Annual Program

How do professional turf managers keep their lawns looking lush? They follow a carefully designed annual lawn care plan. You can do the same thing with your lawn. Start in the early spring, and tackle one step every two months. On an average-size lawn, the whole program requires only about 30 minutes four times a year. The result: A lawn that is the envy of the neighborhood.

1 ***Early Spring (February to late March)***

Apply Scotts Turf Builder Plus Halts® to prevent crabgrass, foxtail, and spurge. It is important to apply this pre emergent plus fertilizer before annual weeds sprout. Turf Builder Plus Halts prevents annual weeds from growing so you will never see these troublesome pests. In the Pacific Northwest, substitute Scotts Turf Builder Plus Moss Control and, in St. Augustinegrass areas, substitute Scotts Bonus® S. These products not only control troublesome moss and weeds, but also give your lawn a good feeding.

2 ***Late Spring (April to June)***

Apply Scotts Turf Builder Plus 2® to kill dandelions and other broadleaf weeds. Turf Builder Plus 2 also provides the right amount of fertilizer to keep your lawn a lush green in late spring. Substitute Scotts Turf Builder if you have a St. Augustinegrass lawn.

3 ***Summer (June to August)***

Apply Scotts Turf Builder Plus Insect Control to keep your lawn green and control more than 22 kinds of lawn insects.

4 ***Fall (September to November)***

Don't forget to feed your lawn in the fall. A fall feeding keeps your lawn greener through winter and quickens green-up in the spring. Apply Scotts Turf Builder for an extended feeding that will thicken your lawn. In St. Augustinegrass areas, substitute Scotts Bonus S to feed your lawn and control weeds.

Scotts four-application lawn programs are easy and economical ways to get professional results. Look for displays of these programs in early spring at stores near you.

Top: Seeding or fertilizing large areas of lawn is accomplished more easily with an appropriately sized spreader.

Center: To keep a lawn flourishing and green, it should be fertilized four times each year.

Bottom: Early morning is the ideal time to water your lawn. Temperatures are cooler, winds are lighter, and the water soaks deeply into the root zone rather than evaporating.

WATERING

As a general rule, most lawns should receive at least 1 inch of water per week, either by rainfall or watering. If watering is needed, it is best to supply about ½ inch of water every three to four days. This usually means leaving the sprinkler in place for about a half-hour at each spot.

Measuring the water. To get a more accurate measurement, simply set out four cans (all the same size) within the sprinkler's range and turn on the water for one hour. Then pour all of the collected water into one can. Measure the water depth with a ruler and divide by four to get the average water output from your sprinkler for one hour. Then adjust your watering time accordingly.

Limited water supply? If watering is limited, remember that a little water is better than none. But don't use your hose and nozzle to sprinkle lightly, because that only wets the foliage, not the soil. Space your waterings so that you can deliver enough water to moisten the soil. Use a sprinkler, but avoid leaving it in one place so long that it causes runoff.

Time of day. Morning is the best time for watering because less water will evaporate and the lawn will have time to dry before evening. The next best time is late afternoon to early evening. Midday is not recommended where high temperatures are common, because of high evaporation then. Nor is watering in late evening or at night suggested, because it encourages lawn-fungus disease.

OTHER LAWN NEEDS

Because lawns are so greatly affected by the environment, there may be other problems that naturally occur from time to time—depending on the whims of Mother Nature. These include weeds, moss, insects, diseases, and thatch.

WEED CONTROL

Lawn weeds have a way of invading a lawn whenever they find an opening. As a result, every lawn requires weed control from time to time—for either one or both of the two major weed categories.

Grassy weeds. Crabgrass is one of several annual grassy weeds that sprouts anew each spring from seeds in the soil. During summer, crabgrass

Dandelions—one of the most common and prolific lawn weeds—are easily eliminated with a weed killer, such as Scotts® Lawn Weed Control.

(and its look-alikes) crowd out the good grass and drop thousands of seeds for an even bigger crop next year. In late fall, with the arrival of the first hard frost, the plants die out.

The only effective way to get rid of crabgrass and its annual cousins is to stop them before they start—in late winter or early spring. This is easily done by applying a crabgrass preventer, such as Scotts Halts®, which forms a barrier at the soil surface and knocks off new crabgrass plants as they sprout—before they can choke out healthy grass.

You may prefer, however, to use a combination product, such as Scotts Turf Builder® Plus Halts, which gives the lawn its early feeding at the same time it prevents crabgrass.

But no matter which product you select, the application must be made early, before crabgrass starts to sprout (generally before the fourth mowing of your lawn in early spring).

Broadleaf weeds. Broadleaf weeds, such as dandelions, plantain, and chickweed, may not be visible in early spring, but by the time the weather warms up, they can become eyesores in the lawn.

TROUBLESHOOTING WITH SCOTTS LAWN PRODUCTS

CHALLENGE	SOLUTION	BEST APPLICATION TIME
Controlled-release feeding	Turf Builder®	Early to late spring and late summer through fall, any time your lawn needs feeding
Growing thick, green turf in the shade	Turf Builder for Shady Lawns	Early to late spring and late summer through fall, any time your lawn needs feeding
Getting new plantings off to a good start	Starter® Fertilizer	Early to late spring and late summer to early fall, any time you plant seed, sod, sprigs, or plugs—or reseed
Seeding damaged areas	Lawn Repair® Kit or Patchmaster®	Early to late spring and late summer to early fall, any time your lawn has bare spots
Safe greening through summer without excessive growth	Summerizer®	June, July, or August
Preparing lawn for winter	Winterizer	Fall through early November
Controlling clover, other broadleaf weeds—and feeding the lawn	Winterizer Plus 2®	Fall through early November
Preventing crabgrass, foxtail, and spurge—and feeding the lawn	Turf Builder Plus Halts® or Bonus S®	Early to late spring, before temperatures are consistently in the 80s
Controlling dandelions, other broadleaf weeds—and feeding the lawn	Turf Builder Plus 2® or Bonus S®	Early to late spring and late summer through fall, any time broadleaf weeds are growing
Preventing and controlling lawn-fungus problems—and feeding the lawn	Turf Builder® Plus Fungus Control	Early spring through fall, anytime disease activity is expected or noticed
Controlling lawn insects—and feeding the lawn	Turf Builder® Plus Insect Control	Early spring through fall, anytime insects are expected or noticed
Controlling moss and developing a thick, green lawn	Turf Builder® Plus Moss Control	Winter through late spring and fall, whenever moss is actively growing
Preventing crabgrass, foxtail, spurge, and other annual grassy weeds	Halts®	Early to late spring, before temperatures are consistently in the 80s
Eliminating dandelions, clover, buckhorn, and other broadleaf weeds	Lawn Weed Control	Early spring through fall, when weeds are actively growing
Protecting lawn from damaging insects	Scotts Insecticides	Early spring through fall, whenever insects are expected or noticed

These weeds can be controlled any time they are actively growing. For best results, treat when temperatures are regularly in the 60s or above. Most homeowners prefer doing the job with a combination product, such as Scotts® Turf Builder Plus 2, which clears out more than 50 weeds at the same time it gives the lawn a full feeding of Turf Builder fertilizer.

Note: For St. Augustinegrass, be sure to use Scotts Bonus® S.

MOSS

Whenever moss is a problem in your lawn, use Scotts Moss Control Granules or Turf Builder Plus Moss Control. See the package for specific directions.

INSECTS

Insects are present in virtually every lawn. Many are beneficial—and the others are often so few in number that they do little damage to the lawn.

When conditions are right, however, the population may become so large it causes considerable lawn damage.

Other insects, such as ants, fleas, and ticks, cause no damage but can be a great nuisance.

The damage. Insect damage generally shows up as patches of browned-out grass. In severe cases (especially with chinch bugs or grubs), the damage is permanent, and the grass will not recover.

Lawn pests, such as white grubs, can ruin the look of even the most well-tended lawn. There are several good products available to eliminate these pests.

Two types. Lawn insects are divided into two categories: surface insects, such as chinch bugs and sod webworms, which do their damage above ground; and subsurface insects, such as white grubs, which damage grass below ground.

The controls. There is a Scotts product that takes care of both surface and subsurface insects: Scotts Diazinon Lawn Insect Control. To clear out insects at the same time you fertilize, there is also Scotts Turf Builder Plus Insect Control. If grubs are a particular problem, Scotts also offers Oftanol* Grub Control.

When to apply. Application of the selected insect control should be made as soon as damage is detected. For grubs, prevention is wise. This can be done by applying the grub control in late spring (April or May) or, more importantly, in late July or early August.

If you carefully follow an annual lawn maintenance plan, you can avoid the myriad blights—such as rust—that detract from your lawn's beauty.

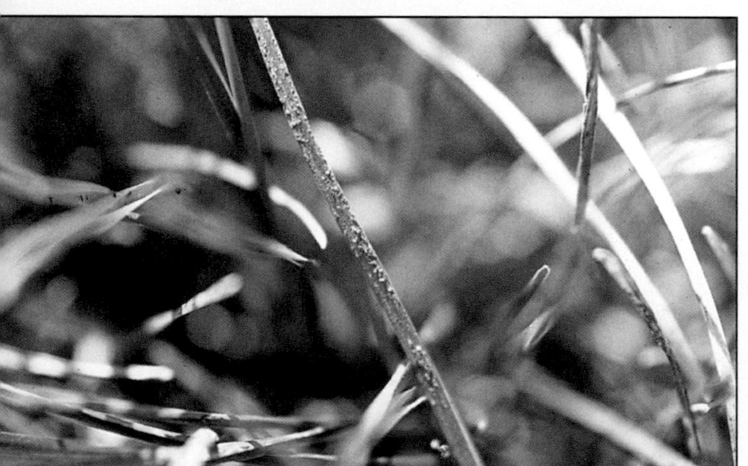

FUNGUS DISEASE

A variety of fungus diseases may attack the lawn from time to time, causing a discoloring of grass plants. Isolated brown areas may result. Upon closer inspection of infected grass blades, you'll find each disease exhibits its own pattern of destruction.

Although there are several of these diseases, most can be controlled by a broad-spectrum disease control, such as Scotts Lawn Fungus Control or Turf Builder Plus Fungus Control. By using either prod-

**Oftanol is a trademark of the parent company of Farbenfabriken, Bayer GmbH, Leverkusen.*

uct on a regular basis, as outlined on the package, you also can prevent disease infestations.

THATCH

Thatch is normal in lawns. It is an accumulation of stems and crowns of dead grass plants that is found just above the surface of the soil. Unlike clippings from mowing, thatch decomposes very slowly. As a result, it can sometimes become thick enough to cause problems.

A modest amount of thatch, ½ inch or so, causes no problems. However, if the layer reaches an inch or more in thickness, the lawn usually begins to show signs of stress.

The problems. A heavy layer of thatch interferes with the flow of water into the soil. It also interferes with the circulation of air around the grass plants as well as the movement of fertilizer and control products in the root zone. Heavy thatch layers also serve as a haven for insects and fungus disease.

The thatch layer can be measured by cutting a plug of turf, thatch, and soil from the lawn. If the thatch layer is 1 inch or more in thickness, the lawn should be dethatched.

A choice of procedures. There are two ways to deal with thatch. The first is to use a power-raking machine, which rakes or slices the thatch material out of the lawn. The machine is operated back and forth across the lawn, like a mower. Several trips should be made, and the thatch should be raked up and removed.

The other method is to use an aerating machine, which removes small cores of turf, thatch, and soil and deposits them on the turf. The resulting holes allow air, water, and fertilizers to work their way more easily into the root zone.

When? Power-raking can be done in spring or fall. Fall is best because the lawn can better handle stress at that time. If reseeding in fall is planned, dethatching should be done prior to the reseeding.

Aerating can be done any time the ground is not frozen. During dry periods, it is best to water thoroughly before starting, to make it easier to remove the plugs.

Equipment availability. Power-raking and coring machines are both available at equipment-rental stores as well as lawn and garden centers.

Fertilize and water. No matter which method is used, dethatching should be followed by fertilizing and watering. This helps the lawn recover from the stress of the dethatching operation and regain its vibrant green color and health. A controlled-release fertilizer, such as Scotts Turf Builder, should be used to stimulate the thickening of the lawn over a long period of time.

If the thatch in your lawn gets too thick to let water and new growth through, rent a power rake or use a heavy rake and dethatch your lawn manually.

PLANTING AND MAINTAINING GROUNDCOVERS

PREPARING THE SOIL

Groundcovers are long-term plantings in the garden, so it's worthwhile to prepare the soil well. Good loam contains lots of organic material, providing plants with the loose, rich soil they need to thrive. Clay and sand are much improved by digging in organic amendments, such as compost, shredded leaves, manure, peat moss, ground bark, or a combination of these. An alternative is to try one of the Scotts® planting soils. They're rich organic blends formulated for specific plant needs.

Cover the soil with a 4- to 6-inch layer of organic material, and work it in to a depth of 12 to 18 inches with a shovel, spade, turning fork, or rotary tiller. Once the soil is turned, rake it smooth, crushing clods and removing rocks.

CHOOSING A GROUNDCOVER

Whether you want quick, low coverage, seasonal bloom, appealing fragrance, or erosion control, there is a groundcover that will serve your needs.

The primary difference between lawns and groundcovers is that most grasses will tolerate substantial foot traffic; most groundcovers will not. Another difference is the fact that many groundcovers provide additional garden color, either from their flowers or from variegated leaves. Groundcovers grown for their leaf color include green-and-white variegated goutweed, silver-and-green yellow archangel, and the bronze-leaved carpet bugle (ajuga) cultivars. Some groundcovers offer an entire season of bloom like the spectacular sheets of color produced by moss pink or brilliantly colored ice plant.

A number of groundcovers grow well in shade, including periwinkle, English ivy, and Japanese spurge. Others thrive in full sun, such as lamb's ears, African daisy, and evergreen candytuft.

Some groundcovers are especially effective for erosion control on slopes and banks, such as star jasmine, trailing lantana, and crown vetch.

Many groundcovers tolerate drought and, in fact, prefer dry conditions. Juniper, ice plant, and trailing African daisy are among the groundcovers that thrive with infrequent, deep waterings. Other groundcovers, such as creeping Jenny (moneywort), mint, and baby's tears, are just the opposite, spreading enthusiastically in moist soils.

Groundcovers that are effective between stepping-stones include Corsican mint, caraway-scented thyme, and Irish moss.

PLANTING GROUNDCOVERS

Most groundcovers are sold in flats, and can be cut into 2-inch squares with a sharp knife. Others are sold individually. Prepare the planting bed before transplanting seedlings into the garden. Hot midday sun can scald or wilt new transplants, so

Above: When groundcovers become overcrowded, divide them and plant them elsewhere in your garden or share them with friends.

Left: Some groundcovers are prized for their bright blossoms, and others for their interesting and variegated foliage. Lamium has both.

Opposite: Sweet woodruff will grow in deep shade. This low-growing groundcover grows rapidly and produces delicate white flowers in the spring.

plant on a cloudy day, late in the afternoon, or a day or two after rain while the soil is still moist.

Immediately before planting, soak the flat thoroughly. Dig shallow holes slightly deeper than the groundcover plugs, fill each depression with water, and let it drain. Place each plug level with the soil and firm the moist soil around it carefully. Leave space between plants for each to spread. Consult your local nursery on proper spacing for the groundcover you've chosen.

Once the planting is done, water gently and thoroughly. Keep soil moist until individual plugs are established and spreading. Use Scotts Transplant Food to get the groundcover off to a good start.

MULCHING

Groundcovers benefit from mulching until they have achieved full coverage. Mulch keeps the soil cooler and moister and helps prevent weeds. It also keeps the groundcover bed looking tidy. Spread a 1-inch layer of organic material, such as compost, shredded leaves, or bark chips.

WATERING

All groundcovers are well served by overhead sprinklers or drip-mist systems on an automatic timer set to a schedule. Groundcovers that like moist soil need regular watering. Those that prefer to dry out between waterings should be soaked deeply but infrequently. Drought-tolerant groundcovers should be watered least often, but watered thoroughly when they are watered. Groundcovers that are not getting enough water signal their thirst by wilting, turning grey-green, or, if succulent, by beginning to wrinkle. All of these signs indicate a plant under stress. Work out the timing so the plant is watered before these signs of stress appear.

FEEDING

Groundcovers grow thicker and lusher when well-fed. Apply fertilizer three times a year. See the chart on page 105 for fertilizer options.

WEEDING

It is essential to keep weeds out of groundcovers while they fill in. Make the job easy by sprinkling Scotts Flower and Garden Weed Preventer throughout the groundcover bed. It's easy to apply, and it prevents crabgrass, foxtail, chickweed, and 24 other annual weeds. Follow package instructions and only use with full-grown plants—not when seeding.

TRIMMING AND SHEARING

Most nonwoody groundcovers can be kept neat and fresh with annual or semiannual trimming to keep them within bounds. Periwinkle looks best if sheared in early spring. Woody groundcovers, such as juniper, cotoneaster, and trailing rosemary, need to have deadwood pruned out frequently. Low-growing groundcovers can be trimmed away from stepping-stones or paved paths with a sharp knife.

PROPAGATING

Many groundcovers root at nodes along the stems. These rooted stems can be cut off and replanted. Matted sections of baby's tears can be trimmed away from stepping-stones and planted elsewhere. Many nonwoody groundcovers can be trimmed into short segments with two or three leaf nodes, laid in a moist seedbed, and top-dressed with topsoil. When kept consistently moist, they will root successfully. Check with your nursery for propagating techniques for specific groundcovers. Once the new plants show signs of growth, feed them to keep them growing enthusiastically.

Answers to Commonly Asked Questions

OVER THE YEARS, THE EXPERTS WHO FIELD CALLS TO THE SCOTTS CONSUMER HOTLINE have answered just about every question that has ever been asked about establishing and maintaining a healthy, vibrant-looking lawn. But there are a few questions that have appeared and reappeared because they are especially good ones. Here they are—and here are our answers. Call us at 1-800-543-TURF, and add your own questions to our list.

Q: When is the best time to seed my lawn?

A: Actually, there are two good times. One is in late winter or early spring, as soon as weather permits. Seeding of thin, established lawns even can be done on frozen ground. For seeding new lawns, the soil must be tilled and dry first. The other good time is in late summer or early fall. Seed will germinate when daytime temperatures are consistently between 68° and 85°F and soil temperature is approximately 55°F.

Q: Is fall a good time to feed the lawn?

A: It's an excellent time! In the fall, grass concentrates its growth in the roots, so your lawn is stimulated to grow thicker and sturdier, instead of longer.

Q: How can I prevent broadleaf weeds like dandelions?

A: You can't. However, Scotts® Turf Builder Plus 2® eliminates weeds after they are actively growing—and at the same time will thicken the lawn to prevent reinfestations. (A thick, vigorous lawn is the best defense against broadleaf weed invasions.)

Q: Why fertilize, when we want to keep grass clippings out of landfills?

A: Not all lawn fertilizers are the same, and they don't all have the same effect on your grass. Scotts fertilizers contain patented slow-release nitrogen to feed your lawn as it needs it, without causing surge growth and necessitating more clippings. Regular Scotts feedings, combined with regular mowing, will allow you to let the clippings fall back onto the lawn, where they will release additional nutrients as they decompose.

Q: I live in a water-restricted area, so I can't water in the fertilizer after application. Is it still OK for me to fertilize in the summer?

A: That's not a problem when you use a Scotts fertilizer. Unlike many other brands, Scotts fertilizers do not have to be watered in. They can be applied any time it's convenient for you. If there's enough rainfall to keep grass growing actively, go ahead and fertilize. But if rainfall is sparse and your grass is brown, delay fertilizing until there's enough rainfall to start the grass growing again.

Q: When is the best time of day to water?

A: The best time of day to water is early morning. If that isn't possible, try late morning, early afternoon, or early evening. Lawn disease proliferates when the sun is absent—so avoid late-evening waterings. Contrary to popular belief, daytime watering will not burn the grass—and, in fact, it actually cools it.

Q: Should I keep children and pets off the lawn after applications?

A: Scotts broadleaf-weed controls work through the leaves of the weeds, so it's important that they stay on the leaves for some time. Scotts recommends that you minimize the use of the lawn for 24 hours after application so that granules will remain on the leaves. Straight fertilizers or crabgrass preventers carry no such restriction. After application of insect controls, water the lawn, and then stay off of it until the grass dries. The weed and insect controls in Scotts products are diluted, so you are not exposed to concentrated chemicals.

Q: How do I know if I need crabgrass preventer?

A: You need it if your lawn had crabgrass or other annual grassy weeds last summer and fall—or just to make certain that it isn't invaded by them this year. If crabgrass preventer has been applied to the lawn for the past two years, and these annual weeds have not been a problem that long, then substitute a straight Scotts fertilizer for the crabgrass-preventer application.

Q: How do I know if my lawn needs four applications per year?

A: The best-looking lawns are those that receive four applications a year. They not only look better, they also improve the environment in important ways. A well-maintained lawn creates oxygen, rids the air of carbon dioxide and other pollutants, traps dust and dirt particles in the air, and controls soil erosion. It also acts as a rain filter to help protect our groundwater.

Q: Can I keep leftover lawn products to use later?

A: Yes. Just roll the top of the bag tightly and tape it closed. Store it in a cool, dry place, out of the reach of children. It's best to use products within three years of purchase.

Plant Alternatives

By using the chart below, nearly every plan in this book can be adapted to fit every climate region. The second column lists the plants that appear in the plans as shown on pages 6-103. Alternatives for designated regions are listed to the right of that column. Plants appearing on the plan pages, but not below, are suited to all three regions.

Plan/Page	Original Plants Listed	Alternatives	
1. Lawns and Borders Pgs. 6-7	<u>Plants for Region B</u> Dogwood (Cornus) Japanese cedar *(Cryoptomeria japonica)* Azalea Lawn: Turf-type tall fescue	<u>Alternatives for Region A</u> Crab apple (Malus) Norway spruce *(Picea abies)* PJM rhododendron hybrid or sheep laurel *(Kalmia angustifolia)*	<u>Alternatives for Region C</u> Evergreen pear *(Pyrus kawakamii)* Norfolk Island pine *(Araucaria heterophylla)* Lawn: St. Augustinegrass
2. Lawns and Borders Pgs. 8-9	<u>Plants for Regions B & C</u> Lawn: Turf-type tall fescue (Region B)	<u>Alternatives for Region A</u> Lawn: Kentucky bluegrass/perennial ryegrass	
3. Lawns and Borders Pgs. 10-11	<u>Plants for Region B</u> Cotoneaster Lawn: Turf-type tall fescue	<u>Alternatives for Region A</u> Bearberry *(Arcostaphylos uva-ursi)* Lawn: St. Augustinegrass	
4. Lawns and Borders Pgs. 12-13	<u>Plants for Region B</u> Climbing yellow rose Ornamental pear Lawn: Turf-type tall fescue	<u>Alternatives for Region A</u> Serviceberry *(Amelanchier laevis)* Lawn: Kentucky bluegrass/perennial ryegrass	<u>Alternatives for Region C</u> Carolina jessamine *(Gelsemium sempervirens)* Lawn: St.. Augustinegrass
5. Lawns and Borders Pgs. 14-15	<u>Plants for Region B</u> Peony Boxwood Azalea *Note: In the coldest parts of Region A, replace celandine with golden marguerites* (Anthemis tintoria).	<u>Alternatives for Region A</u> American arborvitae PJM rhododendron hybrid	<u>Alternatives for Region C</u> Daylily (*Hemerocallis*, evergreen forms) Lawn: St. Augustinegrass
7. Garden Paths Pgs. 18-19	<u>Plants for Region B</u> Variegated goutweed *(Aegopodium podagraria 'Variegatum')* Violet *(Viola odorata)* Lawn: Turf-type tall fescue	<u>Alternatives for Region A</u> Creeping phlox *(Phlox stolonifera)* Lawn: Kentucky bluegrass/perennial ryegrass	<u>Alternatives for Region C</u> Yellow archangel *(Lamiastrum galeobdolon)* Lawn: St. Augustinegrass
8. Garden Paths Pgs. 20-21	<u>Plants for Regions A & B</u> Dogwood (Cornus) *Note: In the coldest parts of Region A, substitute crab apple* (Malus) *for the dogwood, and one of the PJM rhododendron hydbrids or mountain laurel* (Kalmia latifolia) *for the azaleas.*	<u>Alternatives for Region C</u> Orchid tree *(Bauhinia variegata)* Lawn: St. Augustinegrass	
9. Garden Paths Pgs. 22-23	<u>Plants for Regions A & B</u> Climbing rose Serbian bellflower Bergenia	<u>Alternatives for Region C</u> Bougainvillea Creeping phlox *(Phlox stolonifera* 'Blue Ridge'*)* Wild ginger *(Asarum canadense)*	

Plan/Page	Original Plants Listed	Alternatives	
10. Garden Paths Pgs. 24-25	<u>Plants for Regions A & B</u> Dogwood *(Cornus)* *Note: In the coldest parts of Region A, substitute one of the PJM rhododendron hybrids for the azaleas and serviceberry* (Amelanchier laevis) *for the dogwood.*	<u>Alternatives for Region C</u> Evergreen pear *(Pyrus kawakamii)*	
11. Fancy Shapes Pgs. 26-27	<u>Plants for Regions A & B</u> Climbing rose	<u>Alternatives for Region C</u> Blood-red trumpet vine *(Distictis buccinatoria)*	
12. Fancy Shapes Pgs. 28-29	<u>Plants for Region B</u> Colorado spruce *(Picea pungens)* Colorado blue spruce *(Picea pungens glauca)* Campanula Mexican daisy *(Erigeron karvinskianus)* *Note: These species of artemisia are suited to all three regions:* Artemisia absinthium *(Wormwood) and* A. ludoviciana *'Silver King.'*	<u>Alternatives for Region A</u> Feverfew *(Chrysanthemum parthenium)*	<u>Alternatives for Region C</u> Atlas cedar *(Cedrus atlantica)* Blue atlas cedar *(Cedrus atlantica glauca)* Ground morning glory *(Convolvulus sabatius)*
13. Fancy Shapes Pgs. 30-31	<u>Plants for Regions A, B, & C</u> Dogwood *(Cornus)* *Note: The low shrubs bordering the lawn could be replaced with* Ilex crenata *'Helleri' in Regions B & C and* Potentilla fruticosa *in Region A. In the warmest parts of Region C, replace the dogwood with laurustinus* (Viburnum finus).		
14. Low Maintenance Pgs. 32-33	<u>Plants for Regions B & C</u> Pachysandra *(Pachysandra terminalis)*	<u>Alternatives for Region A</u> Purple winter creeper *(Euonymus fortunei var. colorata)*	
15. Low Maintenance Pgs. 34-35	<u>Plants for Region C</u> Mexican orange *(Choisya ternata)* Indian hawthorn *(Rhapiolepis indica)* Mock orange *(Pittosporum tobira)* *Note: In the warmest parts of Region C, replace the ajuga with ground morning glory* (Convolvulus sabatius).	<u>Alternatives for Regions A & B</u> Hills-of-snow hydrangea 'Anthony Waterer' spirea *Spiraea X bumalda* 'Limemound' or 'Little Princess'	
16. Small Space Pgs. 36-37	*Note: In Region C, tulips should be replanted annually or replaced with Persian buttercup* (Ranunculus asiaticus) *or a yellow variety of Dutch iris, either as an annual. In the coldest parts of Region A, the rhododendrons should be the PJM hybrids or should be replaced with mountain laurel* (Kalmia latifolia).		
17. Small Space Pgs. 38-39	<u>Plants for Region C</u> Azaleas Boxwood Lawn: Sonesta Bermudagrass	<u>Alternatives for Region A</u> PJM rhododendron hydbrid or sheep laurel *(Kalmia angustifolia)* Dwarf-winged euonymus or *Thuja occidentalis* 'Emerald Green' Lawn: Kentucky bluegrass/perennial ryegrass	<u>Alternatives for Region B</u> Lawn: Turf-type tall fescue
18. Small Space Pg. 40	<u>Plants for Regions B & C</u> Crape myrtle *(Lagerstroemia)* Lawn: Turf-type tall fescue (Region B) or St. Augustinegrass (Region C) *Note: In the warmest parts of Region C, pink powderpuff* (Calliandra haematocephala) *should replace the crape myrtle.*	<u>Alternatives for Region A</u> Lilac *(Syringa)* Lawn: Kentucky bluegrass/perennial ryegrass	
19. Small Space Pg. 41	<u>Plants for Region C</u> Star jasmine Lawn: Bermudagrass	<u>Alternatives for Region A</u> Three-toothed cinquefoil *(Potentilla tridentata)* Lawn: Kentucky bluegrass/perennial ryegrass	<u>Alternatives for Region B</u> Trailing rosemary Lawn: Turf-type fall fescue
20. Large Space Pgs. 42-43	<u>Plants for Regions A & B</u> English ivy 'Bulgaria' or 'Wilson' Lawn: Kentucky bluegrass/perennial ryegrass (Region A) or turf-type tall fescue (Region B)	<u>Alternatives for Region C</u> Yellow star jasmine Lawn: St. Augustinegrass	
21. Large Space Pgs. 44-45	<u>Plants for Region B</u> Yew *(Taxus)* Welsh poppy *(Meconopsis cambrica)*	<u>Alternatives for Region A</u> Arborvitae *(Thuja occidentalis)* or Canada hemlock *(Tsuga canadensis)* Sulphur cinquefoil	<u>Alternatives for Region C</u> Shrubby yew pine *(Podocarpus macrophyllus maki)* Marguerite *(Chrysanthemum frutescens)*
22. Large Space Pgs. 46-47	<u>Plants for Region B</u> Dwarf conifer Japanese maple *Note: In Region A, the rhododendron should be a cold-hardy type, such as 'Roseum Elegans' or a PJM hybrid.*	<u>Alternatives for Region A</u> Amur maple *(Acer ginnala)*	<u>Alternatives for Region C</u> Shrubby yew pine and fern pine *(Podocarpus gracilior)*

Plan/Page	Original Plants Listed	Alternatives	
23. Large Space Pgs. 48-49	**Plants for Region C** Camellias Pink star magnolia *(Magnolia stellata* 'Rosea'*)*	**Alternatives for Region A** Mountain laurel *(Kalmia latifolia)* or PJM rhododendron hybrid Sargent crab apple *(Malus sargenti)*	**Alternatives for Region B** Rhododendron
24. Large Space Pgs. 50-51	*Note: In Region A, the ornamental grasses should come from winter-hardy types, such as blue oat grass, ribbon grass, or blue lyme grass. Likewise, the winter-hardy pinks should come from types such as allwood pink or maiden pink. In Region C, the pinks will be short-lived perennials. If the daisies are English daisies* (Bellis perennis)*, they, along with the violas, can be handled as biennials or annuals.*		
25. Large Space Pgs. 52-53	**Plants for Regions A & B** Cranesbill *(Geranium sanguineum)* Winged euonymus *(Euonymus alata)*	**Alternatives for Region C** Stokes' aster *(Stokesia laevis)* Heavenly bamboo *(Nandina domestica)*	
26. Large Space Pgs. 54-55	**Plants for Region B** Dogwood *(Cornus)* English ivy Periwinkle *(Vinca major)*	**Alternatives for Region A** Crab apple *(Malus)* English ivy 'Bulgaria' or 'Wilson' Creeping phlox *(Phlox stolonifera* 'Blue Ridge'*)*	**Alternatives for Region C** Orchid tree *(Bauhinia variegata)* Yellow star jasmine Ground morning glory *(Convolvulus sabatius)*
27. Large Space Pgs. 56-57	**Plants for Regions B & C** New Zealand flax *Note: In the warmest parts of Region C, replace the climbing rose with violet trumpet vine* (Clytostoma callistegioides).	**Alternatives for Region A** Soapweed *(Yucca glauca)*	
28. Gentle Slope Pgs. 58-59	*Note: In the warmest parts of Region C, replace the weeping Canada hemlock with Noell grevillea* (Grevillea *'Noelii'*)*; and in the coldest parts of Region A, replace the azaleas and rhododendrons with one of the PJM rhododendron hybrids or mountain laurel* (Kalmia latifolia).		
29. Gentle Slope Pgs. 60-61	**Plants for Region C** Trailing gazania *(Gazania ringens leucolaena)* Bougainvillea Dwarf citrus tree Hollywood juniper	**Alternatives for Region A** Moneywort *(Lysimachia nummularia)* Trumpet vine *(Campsis radicans)* Dwarf apple *Juniperus virginiana* 'Canaerti' or 'Cupressifolia' Lawn: Kentucky bluegrass/perennial ryegrass	**Alternatives for Region B** Aaron's beard *(Hypericum calycinum)* Trumpet vine *(Campsis radicans)* Dwarf apple Lawn: Turf-type tall fescue
30. Steep Slope Pgs. 62-63	**Plants for Region B** Maple Pieris Ajuga	**Alternatives for Region A** Amur maple *(Acer ginnala)* Sheep laurel *(Kalmia angustifolia)*	**Alternatives for Region C** Ground morning glory *(Convolvulus sebatius)*
31. Steep Slope Pgs. 64-65	**Plants for Region B** Wisteria Ajuga (carpet bugle) Maple	**Alternatives for Region A** Clematis	**Alternatives for Region C** Violet trumpet vine *(Clytostoma callistegioides)* Ground morning glory *(Convolvulus sabatius)* Sweet gum *(Liquidambar styraciflua)*
32. Steep Slope Pgs. 66-67	**Plants for Region C** Society garlic *(Tulbaghia violacea)* Trailing rosemary Primrose jasmine (*Jasminum mesnyi*) Mock orange Lily-of-the-Nile *(Agapanthus)*	**Alternatives for Region A** *Allium senescens* Bearberry *(Arctostaphylos uva-ursi)* Cinquefoil *(Potentilla fruticosa)* *Spiraea X bumalda* 'Limemound' or 'Little Princess' *Allium caeruleum* or Stars-of-Persia	**Alternatives for Region B** *Allium senescens* Cinquefoil (*Potentilla fruticosa*) *Spiraea X bumalda* 'Limemound' or 'Little Princess' *Allium caeruleum* or Stars-of-Persia
33. Steep Slope Pgs. 68-69	**Plants for Regions A & B** Euonymus *(Euonymus fortunei radicans)*	**Alternatives for Region C** Yellow star jasmine	
34. Along the Foundation Pgs. 70-71	**Plants for Region B** Liriope (Lilyturf) Boxwood *(Buxus)* Mock orange	**Alternatives for Region A** Carpet bugle *(Ajuga reptans)* Emerald arborvitae *Spiraea X bumalda* 'Limemound' or 'Little Princess'	**Alternatives for Region C** Shrubby yew pine
35. Along the Foundation Pgs. 72-73	**Plants for Region C** Azalea Nandina Weeping fig *(Ficus benjamina)* *Note: In Regions A & B, the fuchsias can be replanted yearly, or they can be replaced with tree roses.*	**Alternatives for Region A** PJM rhododendron hybrids *Spiraea X bumalda* 'Anthony Waterer' Cutleaf weeping birch *(Betula pendula* 'Laciniata'*)* Lawn: Kentucky bluegrass/perennial ryegrass	**Alternatives for Region B** Crape myrtle (*Lagerstroemia indica*) Lawn: Turf-type tall fescue

Plant Alternatives

Plans 23 – 50

Plan/Page	Original Plants Listed	Alternatives	
36. Along the Foundation Pgs. 74-75	**Plants for Regions A & B** Lawn: Kentucky bluegrass/perennial ryegrass	**Alternatives for Region C** Lawn: St. Augustinegrass	
	Note: In the coldest parts of Region A, the hydrangea should be Hydrangea arborescens.		
37. Around Corners Pgs. 76-77	**Plants for Regions A & B** Yew *(Taxus)* Euonymus	**Alternatives for Region C** Low form of juniper or holly Nandina	
38. Edgings Pgs 78-79	**Plants for Region B** Dogwood *(Cornus)*	**Alternatives for Region A** Serviceberry *(Amelanchier laevis)*	**Alternatives for Region C** Evergreen pear *(Pyrus kawakamii)*
39. Edgings Pgs. 80-81	**Plants for Regions B & C** Dwarf periwinkle *(Vinca minor)*	**Alternatives for Region A** Serbian bellflower Lawn: Kentucky bluegrass/perennial ryegrass	
40. Around Young Trees Pgs. 82-83	**Plants for Regions A & B** White birch *(Betula pendula)*	**Alternatives for Region C** River birch *(Betula nigra)*	
	Note: In the coldest parts of Region A, replace the azalea with one of the PJM rhododendron hybrids.		
41. Around Mature Trees Pgs. 84-85	**Plants for Region B** Paperbark maple *(Acer griseum)* Periwinkle *(Vinca major)*	**Alternatives for Region A** Geranium 'Johnson's Blue'	**Alternatives for Region C** Cajeput *(Melaleuca leucadendra)*
	Note: In Region C, the scilla should be Scilla peruviana *(Cuban lily).*		
42. Around Mature Trees Pgs. 86-87	**Plants for Regions B & C** Japanese spurge *(Pachysandra terminalis)*	**Alternatives for Region A** Purple winter creeper	
43. Poor Soil Pgs. 88-89	*Note: In the warmest parts of Region C, the dwarf conifers need to come from these groups:* Chamaecyparis, Juniperus, Thuja, *and* Thujopsis. *Most South African heaths are suited to the dry-summer parts of Region C. For those areas receiving summer rainfall, these heathlike choices should be used: false heather, cigar plant,* Coleonema *'Sunset Gold', and mondo grass.*		
44. Poor Soil Pgs. 90-91	**Plants for Regions B & C** Japanese maple *(Acer palmatum)* Mock orange *(Pittosporum tobira)*	**Alternatives for Region A** Amur maple *(Acer ginnala)* *Spiraea X bumalda* 'Little Princess' Lawn: Kentucky bluegrass/perennial ryegrass	
	Note: The native Coast live oaks can be replaced in other areas with other suitable native oaks or other spreading trees.		
45. Poor Drainage Pgs. 92-93	**Plants for Region B** Azalea Heavenly bamboo *(Nandina domestica)* Maple	**Alternatives for Region A** PJM rhododendron hybrids 'Anthony Waterer' spirea Lawn: Kentucky bluegrass/perennial ryegrass	**Alternatives for Region C** Chinese tallow tree *(Sapium sebiferum)* Lawn: St. Augustinegrass
46. Around Water Pgs. 94-95	**Plants for Regions A & B** Dwarf Alberta spruce *(Picea abies* 'Conica'*)*	**Alternatives for Region C** Shrubby yew pine	
	Note: In Region A, the aquatic iris should be Iris sibirica, *the forget-me-not should be* Myosotis sylvatica, *and the azaleas should be one of the PJM rhododendron hybrids.*		
47. Winter Color Pgs. 96-97	**Plants for Region C** Portugal laurel *(Prunus lusitanica)* Mock orange	**Alternatives for Region A** Blackhaw *(Viburnum prunifolium)* Serviceberry *(Amelanchier laevis)*	**Alternatives for Region B** Silverberry *(Elaeagonus pungens)*
48. Winter Color Pgs. 98-99	**Plants for Regions B & C** Mondo grass	**Alternatives for Region A** Carpet bugle *(Ajuga reptans)*	
	Note: In Region B, replace St. Augustinegrass with a turf-type tall fescue. In Region A, use a Kentucky bluegrass/ryegrass mixture.		
49. High Traffic Pgs. 100-101	*Note: Pindo palm* (Butia capitata) *is the only suitable replacement for Canary Island date palm, but it is hardy only to the warmest parts of Region B. In Region A, use a Kentucky bluegrass/ryegrass mixture for the lawn, and, in Region B, use a turf-type tall fescue.*		
50. High Traffic Pgs. 102-103	**Plants for Region C** Bougainvillea Heavenly bamboo Mock orange *(Pittosporum tobira)* Yew pine *(Podocarpus macrophyllus)* Fortnight lily Lawn: Scotts® PatchMaster® Tall Fescue	**Alternatives for Regions A & B** Wisteria *Euonymus alata compacta* Shrubby cinquefoil (Potentilla) Arborvitae Bearded iris Lawn: Scotts PatchMaster Sun/Shade	

Index

Note: Page numbers in *italics* refer to photographs in which a listed plant appears.

G-K

L-O

P-R

SAVE $2 with $5 minimum purchase

See & Do SOLUTIONS™

Mail-in Refund Certificate

Good on ALL Scotts® purchases including Scotts tools

Cannot be combined with other offers. Offer limited to $2 per certificate.

SEE BACK FOR DETAILS.

SAVE $2 with $5 minimum purchase

Scotts

See & Do SOLUTIONS™

Mail-in Refund Certificate

Good on ALL Scotts® purchases including Scotts tools

Cannot be combined with other offers. Offer limited to $2 per certificate.

SEE BACK FOR DETAILS.

SAVE $2 with $5 minimum purchase

Scotts

See & Do SOLUTIONS™

Mail-in Refund Certificate

Good on ALL Scotts® purchases including Scotts tools

Cannot be combined with other offers. Offer limited to $2 per certificate.

SEE BACK FOR DETAILS.

SAVE $2 with $5 minimum purchase

Scotts

See & Do SOLUTIONS™

Mail-in Refund Certificate

Good on ALL Scotts® purchases including Scotts tools

Cannot be combined with other offers. Offer limited to $2 per certificate.

SEE BACK FOR DETAILS.

SAVE $2 with $5 minimum purchase

Scotts

See & Do SOLUTIONS™

Mail-in Refund Certificate

Good on ALL Scotts® purchases including Scotts tools

Cannot be combined with other offers. Offer limited to $2 per certificate.

SEE BACK FOR DETAILS.

SAVE UP TO $10

Scotts®

GOOD ON ALL SCOTTS PURCHASES

Scotts®

SAVE UP TO $10

GOOD ON ALL SCOTTS PURCHASES

SAVE UP TO $10

See & Do Solutions™ Refund Certificate

Offer limit $2.
Minimum purchase $5.

HOW TO OBTAIN YOUR REFUND:

1. Buy any Scotts product including Scotts tools. Minimum purchase $5.
2. Save your dated cash register receipt.
3. Clip proof of purchase from product package (see illustration at left). Photocopies and facsimiles not accepted.
4. Mail this certificate, the original or a copy of your cash register receipt, and required proof of purchase to address at right. All 3 items must be enclosed to qualify. Certificates cannot be photocopied, reduced, or reprinted. This offer cannot be combined with other Scotts rebate offers.

Mail to: **Scotts See & Do Solutions Refund**
P.O. Box 1074
Young America, MN 55594-1074

Maximum of $20 per name, household, or address.

PLEASE TYPE OR PRINT CLEARLY

NAME ____________________

ADDRESS ____________________

CITY/STATE ____________________ ZIP ________

Offer good only in U.S.A. where not prohibited, taxed, or restricted by law. Cannot be combined with other offers. Please allow 5 to 6 weeks for delivery.

See & Do Solutions™ Refund Certificate

Offer limit $2.
Minimum purchase $5.

HOW TO OBTAIN YOUR REFUND:

SAMPLE

1. Buy any Scotts product including Scotts tools. Minimum purchase $5.
2. Save your dated cash register receipt.
3. Clip proof of purchase from product package (see illustration at left). Photocopies and facsimiles not accepted.
4. Mail this certificate, the original or a copy of your cash register receipt, and required proof of purchase to address at right. All 3 items must be enclosed to qualify. Certificates cannot be photocopied, reduced, or reprinted. This offer cannot be combined with other Scotts rebate offers.

Mail to: Scotts See & Do Solutions Refund
P.O. Box 1074
Young America, MN 55594-1074

Maximum of $20 per name, household, or address.

PLEASE TYPE OR PRINT CLEARLY

NAME ____________________

ADDRESS ____________________

CITY/STATE ____________________ ZIP ________

Offer good only in U.S.A. where not prohibited, taxed, or restricted by law. Cannot be combined with other offers. Please allow 5 to 6 weeks for delivery.

See & Do Solutions™ Refund Certificate

Offer limit $2.
Minimum purchase $5.

HOW TO OBTAIN YOUR REFUND:

SAMPLE

1. Buy any Scotts product including Scotts tools. Minimum purchase $5.
2. Save your dated cash register receipt.
3. Clip proof of purchase from product package (see illustration at left). Photocopies and facsimiles not accepted.
4. Mail this certificate, the original or a copy of your cash register receipt, and required proof of purchase to address at right. All 3 items must be enclosed to qualify. Certificates cannot be photocopied, reduced, or reprinted. This offer cannot be combined with other Scotts rebate offers.

Mail to: Scotts See & Do Solutions Refund
P.O. Box 1074
Young America, MN 55594-1074

Maximum of $20 per name, household, or address.

PLEASE TYPE OR PRINT CLEARLY

NAME ____________________

ADDRESS ____________________

CITY/STATE ____________________ ZIP ________

Offer good only in U.S.A. where not prohibited, taxed, or restricted by law. Cannot be combined with other offers. Please allow 5 to 6 weeks for delivery.

See & Do Solutions™ Refund Certificate

Offer limit $2.
Minimum purchase $5.

HOW TO OBTAIN YOUR REFUND:

SAMPLE

1. Buy any Scotts product including Scotts tools. Minimum purchase $5.
2. Save your dated cash register receipt.
3. Clip proof of purchase from product package (see illustration at left). Photocopies and facsimiles not accepted.
4. Mail this certificate, the original or a copy of your cash register receipt, and required proof of purchase to address at right. All 3 items must be enclosed to qualify. Certificates cannot be photocopied, reduced, or reprinted. This offer cannot be combined with other Scotts rebate offers.

Mail to: Scotts See & Do Solutions Refund
P.O. Box 1074
Young America, MN 55594-1074

Maximum of $20 per name, household, or address.

PLEASE TYPE OR PRINT CLEARLY

NAME ____________________

ADDRESS ____________________

CITY/STATE ____________________ ZIP ________

Offer good only in U.S.A. where not prohibited, taxed, or restricted by law. Cannot be combined with other offers. Please allow 5 to 6 weeks for delivery.

See & Do Solutions™ Refund Certificate

Offer limit $2.
Minimum purchase $5.

HOW TO OBTAIN YOUR REFUND:

SAMPLE

1. Buy any Scotts product including Scotts tools. Minimum purchase $5.
2. Save your dated cash register receipt.
3. Clip proof of purchase from product package (see illustration at left). Photocopies and facsimiles not accepted.
4. Mail this certificate, the original or a copy of your cash register receipt, and required proof of purchase to address at right. All 3 items must be enclosed to qualify. Certificates cannot be photocopied, reduced, or reprinted. This offer cannot be combined with other Scotts rebate offers.

Mail to: Scotts See & Do Solutions Refund
P.O. Box 1074
Young America, MN 55594-1074

Maximum of $20 per name, household, or address.

PLEASE TYPE OR PRINT CLEARLY

NAME ____________________

ADDRESS ____________________

CITY/STATE ____________________ ZIP ________

Offer good only in U.S.A. where not prohibited, taxed, or restricted by law. Cannot be combined with other offers. Please allow 5 to 6 weeks for delivery.